**Business Leaders Are Talking ...**

**The UnConventional Strategist** cuts through buzzwords and frameworks to show what real strategy looks like in practice—built on pattern recognition, judgment, and the courage to act with imperfect information. Drawing from decades of real-world experience, Jay Nakagawa blends sharp insight with candid storytelling to make strategy feel human, practical, and actionable. This is a must-read for product leaders, strategists, and executives who want to think more clearly, anticipate change, and avoid the trap of "strategic theater." It's thoughtful, grounded, and refreshingly honest - exactly the kind of book today's leaders need.

**—Robert Bunchek**
Officer & VP Strategic Intelligence
Fortune 30 company

This book proves what the author says early on: There is *absolutely* no substitute for experience. A product manager, a salesman, a musician, a family man, a trainer, and a leader—Jay has such incredibly varied and wide-reaching experience that his lessons will touch everyone in their corporate career. The book is simultaneously funny, philosophical, practical, ambitious, and with "feet on the ground." This is not a lofty biographical essay by a CEO (or his ghost writer). It is real, wise, and the best testament to how competitive intelligence and strategy work hand in hand in every aspect of business, and in one's career planning.

**—Benjamin Gilad, CEO**
Academy of Competitive Intelligence (ACI)
Co-Founder, Competitive Intelligence Industry

**The UnConventional Strategist** makes it immediately clear why Jay is often referred to as the "OG" of strategy and competitive intelligence by people who actually do this work for a living. He pulls no punches. The lessons are honest, earned, and grounded in real experience. It's just relatable. Jay translates hard-won insights into compelling stories and frameworks you can actually use, all delivered with a sharp, wry sense of humor that keeps the pages turning. Whether you're building a startup, navigating your career, or rethinking what you want the next chapter of life should look like, this is a book you'll find value in.

**—Jason Smith**
CEO and Co-founder
KLUE

**The UnConventional Strategist** is a compelling, sharp, and bold body of work. This is Ben Horowitz with a touch of Adam Grant's practical psychology and Simon Sinek's leadership themes—but more grounded, more specific, and less self-important. Jay's narrative is a gritty, tactical, deeply personal, and surprisingly funny guide to real strategy. He models what good strategic thinking looks like through narrative, humor, and punch-in-the-gut truth bombs.

**—Laurie Young**
Former Vice-Chair
SCIP (Strategic and Competitive Intelligence Professionals)

Jay has always had incredible insight to cut through the muck (and politics) to get to the core of the issues. His book walks through personal strategies on how to build this in your career. It is a joy to read, with stories of success and epic failures, that will keep you smiling and learning.

**—Camberley Bates**
Chief Technology Advisor
The Futurum Group

I've known Jay for many years and often refer to him as a "renaissance man"—a business professional, musician, chef, instructor/lecturer, and now—an author. Jay is one of our favorite lecturers at SMU and students always comment how much they learn from him on our Saturday morning sessions. This book underscores the type of insights Jay generously shares based on his lifelong adventures and experiences. His book is bold and refreshingly honest on what it takes to succeed in today—and tomorrow's—world.

**—Dr. David Jacobsen**
Executive Director, Experiential Learning
Cox School of Business
Southern Methodist University (SMU)

**The UnConventional Strategist** cuts through the noise. Jay dismantles the myth that strategy lives in frameworks and proves it lives in judgment, experience, and the courage to move before conditions are perfect. With stories drawn from real battles—not business school hypotheticals—he delivers a field guide for leaders who want to think clearly and act boldly.

If you're tired of strategic cosplay and ready for something real, this book delivers.

**—Cam Mackey**
President & CEO
International Safety Equipment Association

# the Unconventional strategist

# the Unconventional strategist

Building, Keeping, and Thriving in Your Career

Jay Nakagawa

**The UnConventional Strategist**

Books may be purchased at www.LaneCovePress.com
Lane Cove Press

Development Editing: Judith Briles, The Book Shepherd.com
Editing/Proofreading: Peggie Ireland
Cover and Interior Design:
Rebecca Finkel, F+P Graphic Design, FPGD.com

ISBN paperback: 979-8-9935871-0-3
ISBN eBook: 979-8-9935871-1-0
ISBN audiobook: 979-8-9935871-2-7
LCCN: 2026903979

Business | Leadership | Management

Printed in USA

# contents

# Introduction

I wasn't always a strategist. I was once a kid who couldn't read well, couldn't spell "lugubrious" (still can't), and walked into the wrong room—literally.

Fast-forward a few decades, and I've led a competitive intelligence team at one of the largest tech companies in the world, advised executives on billion-dollar product bets, and learned how to talk to just about anyone—from a surly CIO in the oil industry to a founder clutching a can of Red Bull and dreams of disruption. But none of that happened because I memorized strategy frameworks or learned to love meetings.

It happened because I learned to see patterns, spot blindspots, and (eventually) trust my instincts—even when they weren't backed by a deck. Or perfect data. (Hint: perfect data doesn't exist—get over it.)

This book is for product managers, strategists, marketers, competitive intelligence professionals, brand managers, and leaders who are tired of strategic cosplay. You won't find "five forces" on every page—even though you should know what that is. You'll find true stories from boardrooms and bars, lessons forged in conflict and tacos, and hard-earned truths about navigating business—and life—when everyone else is chasing buzzwords.

Let's begin with the basic truth: most people don't know what strategy is.

And that's exactly where we'll start.

You see, the word "strategy" has been mugged in a dark alley by consultants and buzzword bandits. It's now duct-taped to vague ambitions, posted on intranet sites, and wielded like a lightsaber in meetings where no one really knows what it means.

I've spent most of my career fighting against that kind of thinking. Not from an ivory tower, but from the trenches—building product roadmaps, running competitive intelligence teams, analyzing competitors, and watching in horror as brilliant people made mind-bendingly bad decisions in the name of "strategy." As my old boss, Greg, used to say, "the first rule of business is to stay in business."

My earliest training? It wasn't at business school. It was growing up in a house where money was tight, time was tighter, and learning to listen—really listen—made the difference between trust and chaos. Later, I learned to read despite my dyslexia, manage a team of five kids (yes, five), and negotiate deals with partners who thought I was bluffing. All of that shaped how I think.

And that's what this book is about.

Not strategy as a spreadsheet. Strategy as a mindset. A way of seeing. A way of operating with imperfect information, conflicting priorities, and emotional landmines. This book is a survival guide for those who lead with curiosity and courage in a world that rewards conformity and jargon.

If that sounds like you, you're in the right place.

There's a moment, if you do this long enough—build products, fight for ideas, lead teams—when you realize: you're no longer just solving problems. You're shaping how people think.

I didn't start there. I started in rooms where I didn't belong, working on products that weren't sexy, navigating egos bigger than their budgets, and convincing people to trust a plan they didn't create. I read slowly, rewrote constantly, asked "dumb" questions that turned out to be smart, and learned from every mistake—especially the ones that were mine.

Along the way, I discovered something important: the best strategists aren't the smartest people in the room. They're the most curious. The most observant. The ones who know when to speak and when to shut up. The ones who listen to what's not being said.

This book is a collection of stories, lessons, and frameworks from a life spent connecting dots—between people, products, companies, and moments that didn't seem important … until they were. It's part field manual, part therapy, part bar conversation—meant to help you become the kind of strategist the world actually needs. And having fun playing "bar chess."

It won't tell you what to think.

But it will help you see more clearly—and act more boldly—when it matters most.

You don't become strategic by accident. It's not a workshop. It's not a slide. It's a muscle you build—slowly, awkwardly, and usually after you've fallen on your face a few times. The next section is where we start building that muscle.

part one

# Becoming Strategic

# Author's Note

**The UnConventional Strategist** is about becoming strategic. Have you ever wondered why some people get labeled "strategic" while others, just as smart and hardworking, get stuck as "tactical"? Or why you can read every business book on the shelf and still find yourself blindsided in the real world? Or why some careers accelerate while others stall—even when the talent looks the same on paper?

That's the challenge of becoming strategic. It doesn't happen because you read the right frameworks or memorize the right buzzwords. It happens through awkward starts, wrong turns, and hard-earned scars. Trumpet players don't pick up a trumpet and play a double-high C on day one. It takes hard practice, pushing yourself, and building your range over time.

For me, the lessons showed up in strange places. Carrying a sales bag and realizing quota doesn't care how slick your presentation looks if you can't connect it to customer value. Watching how patience across the table could force a rival to make the first move. Trying something new when everyone else insisted it couldn't be done. And sometimes getting my head handed back to me before regrouping and charging again.

Throughout **The UnConventional Strategist,** you'll see parts of my journey toward becoming strategic in my thinking and approach.

You'll learn ...

- Why perfect kills progress faster than failure.
- Why validation always trumps wishful thinking.
- Why knowing yourself is the ultimate competitive edge.
- Why asking the uncomfortable question no one else will flips the whole game.

And that's not all ... get ready to discover ...

- How fire in the belly separates winners from also-rans.
- How strategy can be born in unlikely places ... yes, even dogs climbing trees.
- How the School of Hard Knocks is still the best teacher.

If the rest of this book is about how to wield strategy, the first part is about things to consider as you move towards being a strategic thinker. Not by declaring it, but by earning it—one scar, one insight, and initiating one move at a time in your own journey.

### The Three Lenses of Insight

Before you can recognize patterns, you have to see clearly—and that's where companies and people tend to struggle.

They confuse data with intelligence and information for insight. That's like mistaking a weather report for a survival plan.

To see what others miss, you need three lenses: one for the landscape, one for the battlefield, and one for the future.

### Strategic Intelligence ... The 30,000-Foot View: the Future

Your long-range radar. Not about the next quarter—it's about the next curve. Strategic Intelligence connects dots others don't even notice. It's about how to get future competitive advantage.

> **If AI regulation shifts and supply chains fracture —what does that do to us?**

These people don't fight fires. They read weather patterns. They keep leadership from steering into icebergs while everyone else argues over deck chairs.

### Competitive Intelligence ... the Knife Fight: the Battlefield

This is where asymmetry lives. Competitive Intelligence (CI) is about anticipation—seeing the move before it's made.

CI pros are detectives and poker players. They spot the quiet job posting, the odd patent, the sudden partnership.

"Why did our rival just hire three pricing analysts in Singapore?"

While others react, CI sees the pattern and sets the trap.

### Market Intelligence ... The Playing Field: the Landscape

This is the rhythm of the market, the voice of the customer, the shape of demand. Market Intelligence (MI) shows where growth hides—and where margins are bleeding out.

"This segment's about to explode, and everyone's looking the wrong way."

They chart where to play, before the analysts do.

### Bringing It Together

- Market Intelligence (MI) shows where to play.
- Competitive Intelligence (CI) shows how to win.
- Strategic Intelligence shows why it matters.

See only one lens and the picture blurs. See all three. When you do, you create asymmetry.

Because it's not the company with the most data that wins. It's the one that sees what's coming, acts faster, and leaves everyone else asking, "How did they see that?"

Becoming strategic begins with learning to see the whole board. Before you master frameworks, you have to master perspective.

Get ready to sharpen your vision with ...

- How to think beyond the noise.
- How to spot what others ignore.
- How to make moves that shift the game.

Strategy isn't a department. It's a discipline of seeing, thinking, and acting differently.

Welcome to **The UnConventional Strategist.**

one

# What It Takes to Win Never Changes

Strategy without execution is theory.
Execution without insight is chaos.

Watching the Stanley Cup Finals, a powerful ad caught my attention. It flashed back through hockey history—from the days before Wayne Gretzky (the Great One), through his iconic era, and into today's fast-paced game. This final message appeared on screen.

### What it takes to win never changes.

It hit me hard—and got me thinking. Instant goosebumps.

Because that truth doesn't just belong on ice—it applies to every boardroom, product, and market battle I've ever seen.

I've watched Super Bowl games since I was a kid, back when half-time shows weren't over-the-top Vegas auditions and quarter-backs still got clobbered without 37 penalty flags flying. Even without knowing all the positions or understanding every penalty call, I could tell who the winning team would be—the one with fire in their belly, a game plan in their head, and a deep belief they weren't just there to play … they were there to *dominate.*

It's no different in business.

After 23 years as a successful product manager, plus 14 years leading strategy and competitive intelligence, I've seen trends rise and fall like overhyped crypto coins. Waterfall. Agile. Scrum. JTBD (Jobs To Be Done). Design Thinking. They all have their place. They all have their cult followers. But *none* of them matter if your product strategy is weak, confused, or completely disconnected from the real world.

Because here's the unfiltered truth:

**Winning isn't about having the best process.
It's about having the right strategy.**

Because what it takes to win never changes. And a half-baked strategy wrapped up in a nice shiny process is still a half-baked strategy.

Or, as I told fellow college students complaining in the dorm food line, "Sorry, I can't make roast beef outta horse's ass."

## A Great Idea Is Not Enough

I've seen this over and over.

A team falls in love with their "big idea," they race off to build it like it's the next iPhone—and ends up in a glorious faceplant. Zero market validation, no real understanding of the problem or what they were solving. A Frankenstein feature list stitched together from imaginary stakeholder wish lists and "wouldn't it be cool if …" fantasies. Welcome to fantasy island.

**Newsflash: Cool doesn't sell
if it doesn't solve something real.**

Chris Tottman, founding General Partner at Notion Capital and coauthor of *The Big Book of BrainDumps* nailed it in a LinkedIn post in mid-August 2025 when he said, *"MVPs don't come first. Problem validation does."* Amen.

Tottman is right. Rushing to build an MVP, a Minimum Viable Product, without validating the actual customer problem is like building a bridge before checking if there's even a river to cross, whether you have the right building materials, and sound architectural design that fits the load requirements. You'll burn time, money, and goodwill. You'll confuse customers. You'll wonder why no one's buying your "brilliant" solution. And you'll start pointing fingers at marketing, pricing, the economy—anything but the real issue: **you skipped the hard part.**

Validate first. Then build.

What's the problem? Who has it? Is it painful enough that they'd pay to fix it? Do they even care? Hint: "that's interesting" is not a buying signal. "Where can I get this?" is.

## Understand the Playing Field or Get Played

Markets shift. Competitors evolve. And sometimes your biggest threat comes from where you least expect it.

Look at what happened to Borders Books. When it outsourced their online store to Amazon, Borders thought it was saving money. Wrong. What it did was seed its demise. What Borders' management really did was give its customers and revenue stream away on a silver platter. The management team outsourced the company's future to its executioner.

**Ignore blind spots long enough and you'll find yourself in a wreck.**

That's not just a mistake. That's a blind spot with catastrophic consequences.

Business blind spots are just like the ones in your car: ignore them long enough, and you'll find yourself in a wreck.

Look at Blockbuster. Its leaders couldn't see beyond the rewind button. They dismissed patterns about digital streaming. Laughed at the offer to purchase Netflix for $50M. They're not around any longer—a classic case of over-confidence bias. Short-term thinking. Epic failure.

My question for you is: Do you understand your market? I mean *really* understand it?

- Who are your current competitors?
- Who are your emerging threats?
- What are the macroeconomic or policy headwinds?
- What about regulatory shifts, tariffs, AI disruption, or new entrants from adjacent spaces?
- What changes are you NOT prepared for?

If you don't have answers to the above—or at least hypotheses—you're doing the equivalent of running naked in the forest with your eyes closed. Guaranteed, the results won't be pretty.

What Makes You a Standout?

This is the question that separates pretenders from contenders:

**How is your product or service truly differentiated?**

And no, "We care more" or "We're innovative" doesn't count. That's fluff. That's what everyone says. That's brochure filler and a yawn to the reader or listener.

- Do you solve a painful problem better than anyone else?
- Do you make something faster, cheaper, smarter, or more delightful than the competition?
- Do customers know that—and *feel* that?
- Are you throwing speeds, feed, and techno-babble specs at them or are you emotionally connecting with something they *need*?

**You can't outspend everyone. But you *can* outsmart them.**

In Daniel Kahneman's *Thinking, Fast and Slow,* he discusses how most people process things using a "System One" and "System Two" construct. System One deals with emotion, and lots of other things, while System Two is the data-driven portion. System Two is never invoked unless System One asks it to get involved. If you never emotionally connect with your message, System Two doesn't care. That's why throwing data about your widget doesn't connect.

## What's your message that emotionally connects with your prospect?

You can't outspend everyone. But you *can* outsmart them. And if your strategy is rooted in deep insight, authentic differentiation, and an ability to adapt faster than others—then you're playing to win. Keep in mind the minute you succeed, someone will copy. Or attempt to copy.

A key point in outsmarting others: you need sustainable differentiation. Something over the long haul. As Tony Fadell, the father of the iPod, iPhone, and Nest products says, the first thing the competition will do is imitate without really understanding requirements. Honeywell tried to take down Nest. When imitation failed, they tried litigation.

What it takes to win never changes. A sustainable strategy means building a moat. Then digging deeper when they try to cross it.

## China's EV Playbook: A Lesson in Strategy

Take electric vehicles as an example. In the US, the average EV costs around $55,000. In China? It's 40% less, closer to $33,000.

And that's not because the quality is lower.

I was recently in Beijing and saw firsthand: China's EVs are luxurious—plush interiors, smooth rides, lightning-fast acceleration. It's what China does best: takes a product, applies economies of scale, and optimizes relentlessly until it can deliver high-quality, affordable alternatives that challenge global incumbents.

Yes, those China EV manufacturers have integrated supply chains, government subsidies, favorable labor cost, and have done their pricing homework. All part of their strategy based on two cornerstones of EV and battery production.

That's strategic execution. That's how you win.

## Did Other EV Manufacturers Anticipate China's Rise?

It is reported that Tesla did and built their Shanghai Gigafactory in 2019 to take advantage of some of the same supply chains and economies of scale their Chinese counterparts were enjoying especially around lithium battery production.

*Harvard Business Review's* "Tariffs and Trade 2025" (May 2025) makes a simple point: companies like BYD and CATL aren't just competing—they're compounding. China's EV market is growing fast, becoming more profitable, and benefiting from a manufacturing learning curve most global competitors simply can't match.

These two companies are structured and focused on their processes and have made rapid advancements that will make it hard for other EVs and battery producers to catch up. CATL is stated to have 38% of the global battery manufacturing capacity (at 15GWh annually). China—overall—is expected to manufacture 4,800 GWh in 2025. This will make it extremely difficult and costly for competitors to try and catch up given their rapid production advancements and economies of scale.

**What it takes to win never changes.**

## Anticipate. Strategize. Execute.

A strong product strategy does more than align your team. It anticipates moves from future competitors, builds defensible moats before they're needed, and helps you adapt in real-time when the unexpected hits.

Think about top golfers like Rory McIlroy, Bryson DeChambeau, or Scottie Scheffler. Each might play the same hole differently because they know their strengths, their competitors, and the conditions. Their strategy is unique, but their **goal is the same: win the hole, win the round.**

Your product strategy is no different.

## Winning Isn't Luck. It's Strategy + Execution.

Winning product strategies don't just protect you—they empower your team.

They help you by:

- Moving faster with clarity
- Staying aligned across teams
- Capitalizing on competitor blind spots
- Adapting without losing focus

Because ultimately, what it takes to win never changes.

What it takes is:

- Deep market understanding
- Strategic foresight
- Flawless execution
- Resilience and adaptability

Winning isn't about luck. It isn't about working more hours. It's not about jumping on the latest buzzword-laden methodology or creating a deck with 47 KPIs (Key Performance Indicators). It's about seeing what others don't. It's about winning with intelligence and imaging the future differently.

And it's about doing the hard things: Understanding the real problem, knowing the market, anticipating competitors, building what matters, and executing with intensity.

Whether you're on the ice rink, golf course, or in the boardroom, it's always game on.

Because what it takes to win never changes.

# key lessons

### 1. Strategy Beats Process—Always.

Frameworks come and go: Agile, Scrum, Design Thinking. The fundamentals of winning never change.

Success comes from a **clear, grounded strategy** that connects to reality, not from dressing up chaos in a new methodology.

A shiny process can't fix a bad strategy. It never has ... it never will.

### 2. Validate Before You Build.

Ideas are easy. Insight is rare.

The difference between failure and traction is **validating the real problem** before building the solution.

Don't fall in love with your idea. Instead, fall in love with the problem you're solving.

### 3. Anticipate, Differentiate, and Execute Relentlessly.

Winning isn't luck. It's the ability to **see what others don't, act before others do, and adapt faster than they can.**

That means anticipating competitors, building moats that last, and executing with clarity and intensity.

Strategy without execution is theory. Execution without insight is chaos.

Winning isn't about luck or the latest framework or jumping on the strategic fad du-jour. It's about showing up with clarity, intensity, and purpose. But clarity without execution is just theory. Just like execution without insight is chaos. Let's get practical.

two

# The Difference Between Knowing It and Doing It

There's a level of knowledge you only get by doing the job … and earning your diploma from the School of Hard Knocks.

Early in my career, I was just cocky (arrogant?) enough to think I could figure out any job from the sidelines. Like how to sell without actually doing it. I was the classic armchair quarterback. With that attitude, I might've made a hell of a corporate consultant, if only I knew how to use "orthogonal" in a sentence.

Thankfully, a mentor set me straight. She told me, "You'll never understand sales until you carry a bag." So, I did. And let me tell you, nothing exposes your ignorance faster than a quarterly quota.

Back when my kids were growing up, "poseur" was their insult of choice. It fit. Had I not sold in the field, I'd have been a sales poseur … faking it with no clue. Turns out, you can't fake quota. At least not for long. Sales poseurs take on the title "unemployed."

As social psychologist and author of *Presence* Amy Cuddy—a fabulous speaker with an incredible story said: "Fake it 'til you become it." She overcame a traumatic brain injury that drastically impacted her cognitive abilities. She was forced to relearn basic skills. At times she felt like she was an imposter. Her imposter mode seeded her groundbreaking research on "power posing," body language, and finding personal power.

So while faking it, just know, you still have to become it.

There's a level of knowledge you only get by doing the job … and earning your diploma from the School of Hard Knocks. I have multiple advanced degrees from there. That's why I chased down different corporate roles. Not to pad a résumé, but because each job gave me something reading about it never could: perspective and experience. There are insights you can only get by doing it via the ingrained learning that comes from hard knocks.

Eventually, I took this curiosity overseas. Different countries. Different norms. Cultural relevance. Different languages. Caste systems and hierarchies. Each one delightful in its own context. And, of course, different "delicacies."

Like the time in Tokyo when my Japanese boss proudly served me sashimi and waited for my reaction. I said it was "very chewy." He grinned, saying, "Uma." Great. Raw horse. I should've neighed and snorted right there.

I also learned some countries' cuisines and my digestive system are natural enemies. One mentor put it simply: "If you can't eat the food, don't go." Words to live and travel by. Believe me, visiting hospitals in foreign countries is stressful. Bottom line: know yourself and your limitations.

**Know yourself and your limitations.**

## Can GenAI Replace Experience?

These days, Generative AI is elbowing its way into everything. But can it actually replace experience—the kind that the School of Hard Knocks delivers?

In a May 2025 *Fortune* article, "Open AI CEO Sam Altman says Gen Z and Millennials use ChatGPT like a 'life advisor.'" Altman pointed out that older folks use GenAI like Google; Gen Xers treat it like a life coach; and Gen Z uses it for… everything. They treat it like an operating system for life: truth engine, therapist, and cheat code all in one.

**Why the gap?**
**One word: experience.**

Older pros lean on lived experience and use GenAI to speed up research. Middle agers are looking to supplement their gaps. And the youngest? They don't have much life experience yet, so they just ask it everything. Worse yet? They believe whatever it tells them verbatim and as gospel truth without question.

**We're outsourcing critical thinking.**

And that makes me uneasy.

Why? Because GenAI isn't infallible. It's fast, slick, confident—and wrong more often than you'd like. It can hallucinate. It makes stuff up. It can parrot biases. And it does all this with the swagger of a TED Talk speaker on Adderall.

It's imperfect because it was built by imperfect people. Just like us.

There's no substitute for experience. Especially the kind that humbles you, scars you a little, and teaches you how to read a room, not just a spreadsheet.

## Consulting Without Consequences

For decades, I had a front-row seat to a very special kind of corporate creature: the **PowerPoint mercenary.** You know the type.

They breeze in with a deck full of arrows, pyramids, and frameworks they downloaded from McKinsey's leftovers. Then they dazzle everyone with words like *synergy*, *cognitive dissonance*, and *disruptive adjacency*. And then the final act, they vanish before anyone notices their recommendations are completely detached from reality.

**It's consulting without consequences.
Strategy karaoke.**

I once watched a consultant pitch a complete go-to-market overhaul to a company whose real problem was it they didn't know how to ship anything on time. Supply chain was a dumpster fire. But hey, at least now the company had a new mission statement.

What I learned is this: **you can never outsource accountability.** Unfortunately, accountability is left for those poor souls left to implement those recommendations after the consultant leaves.

Giving advice is easy. Living with the fallout? Not so much.

That's why I always wanted to take the job *after* the shiny decks were presented. Because doing the job—owning the result, sitting with the consequences, adjusting mid-flight—that's where you actually learn something. Even when it hurts.

Or, especially when it hurts.

## Experience: The Sequel

Experience isn't always fun. Sometimes, the most painful experiences are the most insightful. Sometimes it's delivered by a shouting CIO using colorful metaphors you don't print in a book your mother might read.

Years ago, after an acquisition, we rebilled a customer—a financial giant—for a product they'd already paid for from the previous owner. They were *not* amused. The CIO dragged me and our rep into his office and let us have it for 30 minutes straight. Said we were trying to fornicate him. (He used a different word. See how less offensive it is when using the Latin term?)

I asked him if they had acquired an insurance company that had written policies resulting in losses, wouldn't they force a change to the underwriting and reissue policies based on financial goals that minimized losses? He replied, once again, they would never fornicate their customers the way we were trying to fornicate him.

Like kids in a playground fight, we agreed to return to our respective corners and meet again in a couple of weeks. I can't tell you how much I was looking forward to round two (not).

On the plane ride home, I was looking at a magazine—you remember those things? Printed pages. Color photos. Interesting bylines. Weekly publications. Killed lots of trees.

Anyway, I was reading an article and it discussed how these big, bad insurance companies were not renewing policies in southern Florida based on how hurricane Andrew had decimated people in the wake of its path. The article named a number of insurance companies including the one from earlier in the day and its memorable one-way conversation.

I did what any smartass would do. I tore it out, put a sticky on it the next day with the handwritten note "what say you?" and sent it via USPS to this customer. Almost on cue, the customer phoned me calling me more colorful names with the "how dare you send this to me" conversation. When he was done with his rant, I asked him if he was ready to sit down for round two of the discussions. He calmly replied "yes" and we arranged a date and time to meet.

The next encounter was unlike the first—in a much more positive way. He explained that the real issue wasn't paying money, it came down to the fact that if he had to go to the CEO and board to request an unplanned Capital Expenditure (CapEx) he would get fired since this request would show he couldn't manage his vendors.

*Note: when they say "it's not about the money"... it's* ***always*** *about the money.*

Just like in a Warner Bros. cartoon the proverbial light went on above my head. I now understood the real issue at hand. I made some calls back to HQ and returned to our conversation 10 minutes later.

Essentially, I asked if he could pay for some part from his existing Operating Expenditure (OpEx) budget and then roll the rest into next year's CapEx planning budget. The CIO was shocked and delighted at this offer as he could see that "CIO" would no longer potentially mean "Career Is Over." He was grateful we could come up with a solution that would protect him and his career by being flexible and how we approached the situation with a creative solution.

This experience, for me, was invaluable. I was able to work deals in a similar fashion and helped many CIOs and Directors avoid being fired while still getting deferred revenue for the following year. Without the pain of this experience and the lesson that followed, now seared in my brain, I would have never appreciated the financial side of the issue, nor the problem this acquisition created. This "experience" became another tool in my kit of life.

I learned a lesson: sometimes, the real problem isn't what's said in the room—it's what's *not* said.

You can't learn that from a prompt. That's experience.

And GenAI? I doubt it would've solved that one.

## What GenAI Still Doesn't Understand About Leadership

GenAI is impressive. It can write essays, summarize meetings, recommend dinner spots, and explain the history of Prussian military strategy like a caffeinated librarian.

But leadership? Yeah … not quite there yet. You still need the "human in the loop."

**Leadership isn't a list. It's showing up.**

You can ask GenAI how to be a good leader and it'll give you a lovely list: "Empathize. Communicate. Inspire trust."

**Thank you, Captain Obvious.**

What won't it do?

Walk into a room where morale is in the toilet and figure out who's about to quit.

Notice that your best engineer hasn't said a word in two days because they're quietly burning out.

Or take the heat when a project crashes and *you* have to explain it to a boardroom full of suits who think "Agile" is a personality trait.

Leadership isn't a list. It's showing up. It's knowing when to shut up. It's making a decision with 70% data and 30% gut—and owning it if it tanks.

And when it tanks, GenAI won't be the one called into the exec's office.

You will.

And that's when experience … not algorithms … really matters.

That's the difference between knowing it and doing it.

Now that I've stripped away the illusion that knowledge equates to mastery, it's time to look at what really stops progress. Spoiler alert: it's not a lack of tools. It's the chase for perfection that keeps you stuck.

# key lessons

**1. The Real Story Is Always Between the Lines.**

People rarely tell you the real problem—they hint at it, dance around it, or bury it under corporate politeness.

The real skill isn't listening to what's said.... it's hearing **what isn't.**

Silence, hesitation, body language, budget fears, political landmines—that's where the truth hides.

If you can't read the gaps, you'll miss the game.

**2. The Hardest Lessons Come from the Hits You Didn't See Coming.**

The real breakthroughs don't come from success. They come from the moments that embarrass you, humble you, or force you to get creative under fire.

Those painful moments give you **instinct, intuition,** and **pattern recognition** you can't download.

Comfort doesn't teach. Impact does.

**3. If You Haven't Done the Job, You Don't Know the Job.**

Experience isn't a bonus—it's the **price of admission.**

You earn credibility by **doing the work, taking the hits,** and learning the unspoken rules the hard way.

No scars? **No insight.**

Now that we've stripped away the illusion that knowledge equates to mastery, it's time to look at what really stops progress. Spoiler alert: it's not a lack of tools. It's the chase for perfection that keeps us stuck.

three

# Perfect Is the Enemy of Progress

The truth is, most of us aren't paralyzed by perfection because we're perfectionists.

## Mixing, Fixing, and Never Finishing

There's a classic music biz joke:

**"When are you done mixing a track?"**

Answer: **"Never."**

I learned this the hard way. Back in 2005, I produced an 18-piece big band recording as producer and executive producer. Pro Tools is software that lets you tweak *everything*. Great power. Terrible temptation. Kryptonite for the pocketbook. Changes hundreds of dollars into thousands for the music studio and engineer.

I started with a plan. But soon was trapped in tweak purgatory —nudging notes by milliseconds, obsessing over equalization settings, hunting perfection one knob turn at a time. Studio time ain't cheap. Neither is obsession. Nice if you're JayZ. Bad if you're Jay.

Eventually, I had to call it. "Good enough" wasn't settling—it was surviving. And that lesson? Perfection is the enemy of progress.

Plus, it was a damn good CD.

And, it applies to everything we do.
Especially in business.

### The Train of Perfect Data Will Not Be Arriving

I had a boss who couldn't move without "perfect" data. Needed every decimal, every scenario, every contingency. Meanwhile, the rest of us were waiting for him to make … *any* decision.

Paralysis by analysis.

Around this time, I inherited a product so unpopular it practically came with its own warning label.

- **Too expensive:** Built like a tank. Priced like a Ferrari.
- **No demand:** Couldn't get our sales channel interested at all.
- **Zero differentiation:** You'd get more excitement from a cinder block.
- **Dominant competitor:** 80% of the low-end market. 0% of the high-end (where we lived). And they wanted our lunch. Badly. Today.

Boss's advice? Focus on "speeds and feeds." Translation: polish the turd. Response from the sales channel: crickets.

So, I did what any battle-hardened product manager does when cornered: **I got strategic. And scrappy.**

### Insights Are Fuel. Use Them.

This wasn't a product play. It was a war game. I studied the competitor—deeply:

1. They *wanted* the high end. Badly.
2. They *thought* they owned the commodity end, and mostly did.
3. They *assumed* the same playbook would work upmarket.
4. They *lacked* the real-world capabilities to get there.

Found their weakness: They didn't build for high availability (HA). In data centers, HA is gospel. You expect your system to stay up—even if a component goes down. And because we came from the high-end of the market and data center infrastructure, we built serviceability into the products without giving it a second thought and that automatically got carried over in the software to our commodity product line.

Their product? Needed a full system shutdown for service.

Ours? Swap parts while the rest keeps humming.

**Their car gets a flat?**
**Stranded until the car gets replaced.**

**Ours?**
**Pull over, change the tire, keep going.**

Flipped that "minor feature" into a major differentiator. And when we told the story right, IT buyers came running and buying by the truckloads. Literally.

### The Power of the Pivot

We surged from **9% to 50% market share** in record time of several short years.

Our competitor? Blindsided. They'd thrown every engineering resource at winning the high-end ... and left their core exposed. Classic case of leaving the back door unlocked while you siege the castle.

Ironically, in the process, we may have launched the industry's first **capacity-on-demand** product.

And here's the kicker ....

## The Real Mic Drop

The final blow? We had **2 times the capacity** of our rival. Sounds great—except it also made us 2x **more expensive.**

So, we turned the story again:

**"You don't need to buy it all upfront.**

**Pay half the price. Grow as you go."**

**Capacity on demand.** Instant differentiation. Irresistible offer.

That combo of insight, adaptability, and speed?
It beats perfect every damn time.

Customers and sales channel we tested our messaging with loved it. It appealed to Kahneman's System One first: emotional benefit, and justified the purchase with System Two: logic—pay half now and add as you grow. The magic winning combo.

**Mr. paralysis-analysis couldn't pull the trigger.**

But this pay-as-you-go was foreign to the company. We were accustomed to getting all the cash up front. This half-price and pay-as-you-grow meant taking less up front but getting the full dollars over time, forecasted to be 15-18 months after initial purchase.

## Nudge Theory at Work

When I was selling this concept internally, I worked all the key stakeholders and executives to understand the benefits of what I wanted to do. This was long before Richard Thaler and Cass Sunstein would publish their book, *Nudge: Improving Decisions About Health, Wealth, and Happiness,* but their concepts along with Kahneman's framing were at work.

The combination of releasing a very "sticky" product that would lock out the competition and assure a future revenue stream was framed in discussions that overcame the historic status quo of expecting all the money up front.

The executive management committee bought into it with my financial projections and market share forecasts. Even the analyst started liking us again.

However, my boss didn't like the idea. Mr. paralysis-analysis couldn't pull the trigger.

He had people go behind me to verify. And, they said my numbers and projections were spot-on target. But he still didn't think he had all the data he needed to pull the trigger.

Eeyore wouldn't relent. So, they put him out to greener pastures. Oh, bother.

**You see, perfect is the enemy of progress.**

The train of perfect data doesn't exist, makes no stops, and carries no cargo.

## The Exit Music (and a Little Wisdom)

The truth is, most of us aren't paralyzed by perfection because we're perfectionists.

We're paralyzed because we're afraid—of getting it wrong, of being blamed, of launching something that flops harder than a one-hit-wonder's comeback tour. But here's the kicker: progress doesn't come from waiting. It comes from moving—strategically, imperfectly, guts, and sometimes with a bit of duct tape and luck.

If I had waited for everything to be perfect, we would've missed the market, missed the opportunity, and missed our moment. Instead, we got scrappy, told the right story, and won. Not because we had the best product, but because we had the best *insight* and the courage to move. It also gave us time to develop the next generation with a bill of materials in line with the commodity market.

So, the next time you find yourself endlessly tweaking the plan, chasing flawless data, or polishing a PowerPoint deck for the 47th time—remember this:

**Progress doesn't wait for perfect.**
**And neither should you.**

The final mix of the music is "good enough." Ship it. Test it. Learn fast. Move faster.

And if it's not perfect? Good. Perfect never comes.

But learning this is a step in the direction of learning the art of strategic patience.

# key lessons

### 1. Perfection Is Just Procrastination in a Fancy Suit.

Let's be real: nobody's chasing "perfect data."

They're chasing **an excuse not to decide anything**.

If you need every variable nailed before you act, don't call yourself a leader—call yourself a **very expensive** speed bump.

Meanwhile, the market isn't waiting for you to finish your spreadsheet therapy session.

### 2. Insight Isn't Optional—It's the Only Thing Keeping You from Losing.

You didn't win because your product was a masterpiece; you won because you weren't delusional.

While everyone else was polishing their sad little turds, you used actual competitive insight and, shockingly, **won**.

Newsflash: customers don't buy "perfect." They buy **value + clarity + "holy crap this solves my problem."**

Specs don't close deals. Stories do.

### 3. Courage Beats Cowardice—But Cowardice Loves Meetings.

The people demanding "more data" aren't being strategic —they're being scared.

Their goal isn't progress. Their goal is **not getting yelled at**.

If you wait for perfect conditions, perfect alignment, perfect certainty, enjoy your permanent residency in the Land of Missed Opportunities.

Winners ship.

Cowards stall. It's not complicated.

four

# Strategic Patience: Waiting Without Losing

Once you realize perfection is a trap, you're free to learn, iterate, and lead.

Part of my journey toward strategy was learning the fine art of **strategic patience**—and how to turn it into a weapon.

Back in the late '80's, the gospel was that doing business in Japan took time—a lot of it. The average for an American or other non-Japanese company to land a serious deal? Five years. That was "just the way it was."

I didn't have five years. Hell, I didn't even have three. As the head of business development for the Pacific Rim, my orders were clear: get something signed *fast*—ideally less than two years.

I didn't just beat the timeline. I signed an OEM deal with a major Japanese brand in **18 months.**

## Finding My Sensei

When I first started on the Japan deal, I knew embarrassing little about Japanese business practices. I did what I've always done. I called someone who did.

One of the top high-tech companies in Metro Denver area had a guy who'd cracked the Japan code for getting a deal done in under two years. I called him up cold.

That's one of my strengths—or weaknesses—I'll call anybody. I once rang the author of a mega-bestselling business book just to ask him a few questions. This was the days before email and the internet. He was stunned I'd found his number. Another time, I called a famous Australian composer. He was … less than thrilled. That's usually the exception, not the rule.

Gene, the Japan business veteran, became my guide. Over several weeks, he walked me through the keiretsu networks, trading company politics, and the unspoken rules of doing business in Japan. When I had questions or wanted to strategize, Gene was there.

**If patience was their weapon, I'd turn it back on them.**

## The Japanese Playbook

Japanese companies are the masters of strategic patience. They'll move the chess pieces slowly, partly to test your staying power, partly to position for the best terms. Deals move at a glacial pace—until they don't.

The gatekeepers? The sōgō shōsha (総合商社)-general trading companies like Mitsubishi, Mitsui, Itochu (formerly C. Itoh), Sumitomo, and Marubeni. They brokered business for foreign firms and loved exclusivity like Americans love Super Bowl commercials.

## My Countermove: Reverse Patience

If patience was their weapon, I'd turn it back on them.

Here's how: I approached three major trading companies that showed interest in our product. Each wanted exclusive rights. I kept the conversations parallel—never committing, always hinting.

This was the age of fax machines, WordPerfect, and long-distance calls that cost more than lunch. The faxes flew back and forth like carrier pigeons on steroids. Every few months, they'd fly in for "relationship building" meetings. In reality? Surveillance. They wanted to size us up, literally.

And I could feel it—the quiet competition between them.

## Pressure in the Air

By month 15, each of the three were "making progress" to locking down a partner for us in Japan. That's when I "accidentally" let it slip to each one that there were other sōgō shōsha interested in our business.

You could almost hear the gears grinding across the Pacific, along with the hissing intake of air.

The famously patient Japanese negotiators suddenly sounded like an American sales rep on the last day of the quarter:

- "We'd like to conclude a deal."
- "How can we speed up this process?"
- "What terms do you need us to take to the partner?"

Now the tables had turned. They were pushing for speed; I was dragging my feet.

Every meeting was a dance—smiles and tea on the surface, quiet urgency underneath. They didn't want to lose, but they didn't want to tip their hand either.

I held the pause for two more months and let the pressure build.

## The Decision

Month 18. The bids—formal and informal—were on the table. It came down to who could deliver not just market access, but the best long-term relationship, support, and product margins.

I made the call. One trading company's partner would get the OEM rights to our product in Japan—exclusive to their market. The others? Out.

The deal was signed. And with it, we cracked the Japan code in record time.

**The Lesson:** Patience isn't just about waiting. It's about *making* others wait until they're ready to move on your terms. Used right, patience can close a deal faster than rushing ever will.

## Why It Still Matters Today

The tools have changed—Zoom instead of faxes, WhatsApp instead of telex—but the game hasn't. Whether it's global supply chain negotiations, M&A courtships, or strategic partnerships in emerging markets, the ability to manage time pressure is still one of the sharpest levers you can pull.

Everyone's in a hurry now. That's what makes patience an even bigger advantage. If you can stay calm while the other side starts to sweat, you're already halfway to winning.

> **They didn't like the cost of honoring the agreement.**

Sometimes patience isn't enough—sometimes you have to pull the pin entirely and see who scrambles.

## The Power of Walking Away

Sometimes the smartest strategic move you can make is to pack up your toys and go home.

Same company, different market. This time one of our international partners—not Japan—was struggling with our product line. The problem wasn't in their selling motion; it was post-sales service.

When you bring on a new partner, you expect some ramp time. But they'd signed up for our business model, which required post-sales support: training customers, troubleshooting (rare), and billing for normal annual maintenance contracts. They liked the high margins. They didn't like the cost of honoring the agreement.

## The Meeting from Hell

I flew in for a heart-to-heart. Instead I got a two-hour complaint monologue. They griped about our products, their customers, the local economy ... even the local zoo. Not joking.

I said nothing. Just listened. Inscrutable.

Technically, they were in breach. And I'd heard enough.

As I stood to leave, I calmly said, "I'll have our legal team send you a termination notice." Then I walked out.

Two days later: a frantic voicemail was left. "We need to talk."

I waited two more days before calling back.

When we finally spoke, it was like a leopard had traded all its spots for stripes. No complaints. They'd hired four people for post-sales service and an additional clerk for maintenance billing. "We're ready to do this right."

I told them I would think about it.

## The Chase

Three more days passed. Multiple voicemails from them, multiple times a day.

When I finally returned the call, they were relieved to hear we'd keep the partnership. And from that day forward, they never complained again.

**The Lesson:** Walking away isn't quitting. It's shifting the power dynamic. When the other side realizes the deal matters more to them than to you, they'll move mountains to keep it alive.

## The Last Minute Contract Switch

Another company, another OEM deal. This time with the market leader in their space—a partner already sending us a steady stream of customers for operational planning work using our software. The problem for us was we were small and they were big. Very big.

One day, I pitched a bigger play: OEM our product, fold it into their professional services offering, and make some serious money scaling it. We would serve as their "level 3" support handling the most serious and technically challenging situations. Win-win for both teams.

Over the next couple of months, I built the business model, ran the numbers, and handed a pro forma showing exactly how profitable it could be at different customer volumes. The math wasn't in question. It was just a matter of how far they wanted to push it.

Training their team to deliver was straightforward: get the customer data, load it into our software, model the different operational loads, hand back a plan for current and future operational capacity. Easy money.

## The Silence

Everything was on track—until it wasn't.

Suddenly, radio silence. Calls went unanswered. Messages vanished into the void. In business, that's rarely good news. Might not be bad. But unknown. Something was up.

This was another test of strategic patience. I called just enough to signal I was still interested—but never enough to become a pest. You can't let insecurity drive your dialing finger.

And, while I was waiting, I started quietly building Plan B—taking the same business model to their largest competitor.

## The Pivot

Their competitor moved fast. We'd already done the planning and financials, so the ramp-up was quick. The talks were moving forward while my original prospect stayed silent.

Then, weeks later, the original partner reappeared—wanting to "present a counterproposal." We listened politely, moved toward signing … and at the eleventh hour, they tried to slip in new terms. Terms that were *not* in our favor.

We stalled. For three weeks, we let them sit with their changes while we pushed their competitor's discussions further.

And we made sure they knew we were "exploring other options" after their long silence. In an industry this porous, word travels fast.

When they found out we were working the same deal with their biggest rival, their pace changed overnight. Suddenly, they *had* to the get contract signed—on our original terms.

They knew if we went with their competitor, it would cost them—thought leadership and their reputation of innovation.

**Lessons Learned:** Patience under pressure plus the willingness to walk away doesn't just protect your position. It forces the other side to protect it for you.

When you control the clock *and* the exit, you control the deal. And sometimes, that same instinct—knowing exactly when to press—also tells you when to walk away entirely. Which brings me to one of the clearest "fold 'em" moments.

## The Gambler

If *The Last-Minute Contract Switch* was about holding your ground until the other side blinks, this one's about the flip side of that coin: knowing when to walk away before you're dragged into someone else's disaster.

Kenny Rogers said it best in his hit song, "The Gambler" and knowing when it's time to fold your hand of cards. Business is no different. It's not always about fighting for the win; sometimes it's about spotting the moment when winning isn't worth the cost.

The leader of one of the organizations I belonged to quit—abruptly. Privately, he told me why, but the upshot was that I inherited his job for the interim *and* the unenviable task of finding his replacement.

We followed the same hiring criteria that was used for the well-liked, highly effective leader we'd just lost. I pulled together a lean but balanced search committee: our own team, selected key partners, an outside voice for objectivity, the parent company's rep, and yes, my predecessor himself. Small enough to make decisions, big enough to get real feedback.

The recruiter brought seventy candidates. We narrowed it to twenty. Then to five. And … nothing. Not a single good fit.

It was time to go hunting myself and found two that looked promising. We put them through the gauntlet:

- **Internal team?** Yes. (Except for my predecessor)
- **Partners and outsiders?** Yes.
- **Parent company rep?** Yes.

One candidate emerged as *the one*. All lights green—except for the one red blinking light.

My predecessor had suddenly decided he wanted the job. Never mind that he had *no* managerial experience and wouldn't have made it past his own hiring standards. He went straight to the parent company's rep and made his pitch.

Next thing I know, I'm being told he's getting the job. No explanation that made sense. Just corporate politics in its purest, ugliest form.

I could see the iceberg 100 nautical miles away. And I wasn't about to be part of the band playing on the deck. I folded my hand, handed in my resignation, and walked.

Sometimes, the smartest strategic move isn't to win—it's to make sure you're nowhere near the table when house burns down.

And, once you realize perfection is a trap, you're free to learn, iterate, and lead. But to lead, you need to understand what's driving you. It's time to get to know the strategist. Enter the Oracle.

**The two most powerful warriors**
**are patience and time.**

—Leo Tolstoy, *War and Peace*

# key lessons

**1. Patience Is a Power Play—Not a Pause.**

Strategic patience means you're not waiting ... **you're letting them sweat.**

When you control the pace, you control the deal. Patience isn't passive—it's pressure.

**2. Walking Away Forces the Truth Out.**

Nothing exposes real priorities like telling someone, "We're done here."

The second you're truly willing to walk, people stop posturing and start performing.

Distance is leverage. Use it.

**3. Leverage Comes from Controlling Time, Pressure, and Options.**

Slow when they rush. Accelerate when they stall.

Make them feel the clock, feel the competition, and feel the risk of losing you.

Master those levers and you don't "negotiate": **you dictate the terms.**

And, once you realize perfection is a trap, you're free to learn, iterate, and lead. But to lead, you need to understand what's driving you. So let's get to know the strategist. Enter the Oracle.

five

# Know Thyself ... and Quit Drinking Your Kool-Aid

You can't ship a feature in three days when legal still thinks "Agile" is a personality type.

If you've seen 1999 movie, *The Matrix,* you know the scene: Neo walks into the Oracle's kitchen, sniffing cookies and confusion, and right above the doorway is that cryptic little plaque:

**Temet Nosce**
—Know Thyself

It's subtle. It's ancient. And it's the whole damn point. And you should know: self-awareness isn't just for yoga retreats.

The Oracle doesn't tell Neo he's "The One." She sizes him up, sees he's not ready, and gives him just enough of a push (nudge) so he figures it out himself. She knows that kind of truth has to be discovered, not handed out like free swag and tchotchkes at a tradeshow.

The Oracle says, "Being The One is just like being in love. No one can tell you you're in love. You just know it. Through and through. Balls to bones."

And that got me thinking.

## Most Companies Don't Know Themselves—They Know Their Slideware

I've worked with companies that say they're agile, visionary, the future of [*insert industry here*]—and they believe it. But walk through their processes and it feels like trying to run a marathon in molasses. Or swimming wearing a straight jacket. Everyone's nodding in meetings, repeating catchphrases like "fail fast" and "customer obsessed," but forbid someone actually challenges the status quo. That's when the PowerPoint shields go up and the corporate antibodies rush to kill those with legitimate alternative points of view. "Fail fast"? Why fail at all?

"Denial is more than a river in Egypt"—it's true. And it seems to be endemic in larger companies.

Then there are the big companies who think they're scrappy. They imagine they can move like a startup because they put Cornholes into a conference room, give everyone Slack access and free food. That's cute. You can't ship a feature in three days when legal still thinks "Agile" is a personality type.

And forbid you tell them the truth about that turd on the table. As author Rishad Tobaccowala of *Rethinking Work* so famously says, "It is something that is brown and moist, and people know it is a piece of poisonous waste, but they pretend it is a brownie."

If everybody knows that it's not a brownie, at least not a good kind, why don't they say something?

Rishad explains it usually stems from several fears ranging from being punished, being wrong, being asked to do more work, and being disliked. How often do you see the "Big Kahuna" in the room bully everyone else to accept their point of view? Or watch people passively accept the premise the data is correct without ever challenging it for fear of reprisal? Or fear they will say something that becomes a career-limiting event?

Incidentally, these are the same companies that preach the need for people to "take the initiative," "take risks," and "display courage." And when they do, they find out they are Wiley E. Coyote in a Road Runner episode about to get smashed by the corporate anvil coming down on their heads. With this type of contradictory behavior, is it any wonder why companies run into trouble?

**It's like using a leaf blower to dry your hair. Technically possible. Mostly dangerous. Pretty dumb.**

This is not an indictment on all large companies, but it seems to be more prevalent in those. My advice when you see these types of things going on—run away! Quickly and without regrets.

Avoid the endless stress of layoff bingo as they try to shrink their way to profitability to recover from the bad decisions they've made.

## Stop Pretending You're Something You're Not

This isn't about being small or big. It's about being **honest.** You wanna move fast? Great. Can your teams actually make decisions without five levels of signoff? You wanna be customer-led? Awesome. When was the last time anyone talked to a real customer? Or validated those requirements in your MVP with real customers willing to pay real money? Unvalidated MVPs can lead to disaster and I've seen it happen—science projects that severely damage a company, its reputation, its credibility, and dries up the revenue stream faster than a bowl of water in Death Valley in the Mojave Desert at noon.

Pretending to be something you're not only wastes time, but burns people out, and creates a reality distortion field where nobody can tell the difference between ambition and delusion.

It's like using a leaf blower to dry your hair. Technically possible. Mostly dangerous. Pretty dumb.

This reflects back to the problems when executives become isolated. And it compounds itself when they only surround themselves with people who are active members of their own echo chamber. They start to believe their own press releases and this is reinforced by people who tell them they are great, despite the flashing red signals from the marketplace. They often miss the competitors hiding in the bushes who are cheering them on to "push the pedal to the metal" as they approach the edge of the cliff at 100 mph with not a brake light in sight.

Often, miscalculated executive visions are to blame. Poorly articulated, contrary messages, and when things fail the blame-storming begins in a hunt to exterminate both the guilty and innocent.

I worked at a company where the CEO (admired for his vision) ignored warnings from product management and analysts—trusting only his inner circle. A few short years later, we were circling the drain, sold in a fire sale, and handing out pink slips like they were going out of style.

As one of my friends so infamously answered when asked about this executive peer of his and this person's "vision."

**He replied,**
**"Vision without execution is called delusion."**

## Small Doesn't Mean Weak. Big Doesn't Mean Smart.

I saw a viral thread on LinkedIn around April 29, 2023, that invoked a debate when a member posted a graphic of many of today's consumer brands that showed them as being a part of large conglomerates and in the hands of a dozen or so companies and crying the "little guy" was, for all intents and purposes, dead.

A response by GetFresh Ventures' Founding Partner, Diraj Perkash Goel, forcefully rebutted,

> The small guy is definitely not dead. The small guy builds **segmentations** based on customer evolution and needs. The small guy finds opportunity and expands within that segment with a goal to prove demand, scalability, repeat purchases, micro niche domination, and clear market share ownership that encroaches deeply on a key strategic market segment for the big guys.
>
> The big guys are there to consolidate and bring **economies of scale** on manufacturing, distribution and presentation. Product innovation doesn't happen at the edges of the big guys' machine.

Diraj nailed it. He basically said: look, the small guys aren't dead. They just play a different game. They listen better. They move faster. They find weird little cracks in the market and own them. They build, adapt, learn. The big guys? They're great at distribution and polish. But invention? That usually starts somewhere scrappy.

**Translation:**
**the small guys know who they are.**

The big guys **think** they know who they are … until someone eats their lunch with a fork made of duct tape and spite.

These are the same big companies that are losing market share quarter over quarter but still believe they are the market leaders and innovators.

## Self-Awareness Is a Strategy

"Know thyself" isn't just some dusty Greek saying. It's a survival skill.

Whether you're running a company, a team, or just trying to figure out if you should actually hit send on that email to your boss. Knowing what you're good at, what you're bad at, and what's just not your lane makes all the difference.

It's about understanding your own strengths and weaknesses. Do you like talking with people or are you a reluctant introvert who ends up exhausted after a meeting with other people? Do you like corporate politics or would you rather be left alone to get your work done? Know what you like, dislike, and how it will affect your career. These are conscious and deliberate decisions you should make.

**If you really don't enjoy it, stay away from it.**

Get feedback from your peers and friends who will be honest with you. They want to see you succeed and so does your manager. They need to understand you and your role and job.

We're all mature enough to recognize corporate politics is a reality of business life. But if you really don't enjoy it, stay away from it. You know the warning signs. The beads of sweat. The awkward social feeling. If you do, you've got self-awareness and that will serve you well—in business as well as in life. But what about those who either lack or have a recessive self-awareness gene?

Lack of self-awareness isn't just annoying—it's expensive. It leads to bad bets, bruised egos, wasted effort, and long meetings that should've been a group chat. Trying to coach someone who lacks emotional intelligence, sometimes called "EQ," is a crapshoot if you're a manager. My experience is about 70% of the time, they are incapable of changing. Especially if they belong to an age group where they no longer get carded at the liquor store.

Part of it is nature vs nurture. Occasionally, it is truly being unaware and making the decision to change. Change is hard. Change is uncomfortable. But—sometimes—change is necessary.

As a manager, coaching someone that lacks EQ is a bit like making fresh orange juice. You have to determine if the juice is worth the squeeze. Sour orange juice doesn't taste good.

So my advice is skip the delusion. Skip the ego. Figure out who you are, what you can actually do, and go do that with your whole being. Whatever it is. Be authentic to yourself. Have a career that makes you happy because you don't get a second chance at life and the ability to change the script.

**Pretending you're someone else?
That never ends well.**

## How Do I Find a Good Company?

Good question. It's very much like how do I find a good person to marry and spend my life with?

A good company isn't perfect. It's just one that aligns with your values, sense of pace, ethics, and sanity. And, like relationships, sometimes the best ones aren't the flashiest. They're the ones that show up on time, tell the truth, and make you feel like you belong.

You want to know how a company treats people. In addition to the ones on payroll, find the ones that left. Or the ones that were pushed out. You want to understand the good, bad, and ugly.

**There's an old saying:
Love is blind, but the neighbors aren't.**

Translation into business terms: *Glassdoor isn't gospel, but trends don't lie.*

Make your own observations and watch the trends. Dysfunctional syndrome doesn't just suddenly appear. It comes slowly over time and eats at the very cultural fabric that made a company successful and liked earlier. Policy changes and how employees are treated can—and do—change over time. If a company's reputation goes from great-to-bad, it's a sign the movie you're watching isn't very good. Go find another movie to watch and grab some more buttered popcorn on your way.

I remember being recruited for a company that had a horrible reputation. Didn't treat its people well, full of egotists, and was the poster child for dysfunction.

This happened during the time I was laid off and decided having a job and income beat the alternative. I interviewed and accepted the offer. I remember telling my wife, Veronica, "I'd be surprised if I stayed three months" based on its reputation. Much to my surprise this smaller group within the company was great, had a vision, leadership, and actually let me do my job. Plus, I had a great boss and we're still friends today. Long-story-short, I ended up staying for a number of years having a great career.

So while the book's cover might be tattered, read the reviews on the story it conveys and then read it for yourself. You just might have found a treasure like I did.

## The Final Truth Bomb: Know Thyself—or Risk Becoming a Cautionary Tale

Here's the raw, unfiltered truth: if you don't know who you are, what you value, or what kind of game you're playing—you're not leading. You're just reacting. And reaction without reflection is the highway to irrelevance.

I've seen too many smart people flame out because they drank their own Kool-Aid, believed their press releases, surrounded themselves with yes people, and built slide decks that read like buzzword bingo instead of real strategies. They confused confidence for competence. They mistook title for talent. And when the market reality finally showed up with a folding chair sports entertainment style, they never saw it coming.

But here's the upside: self-awareness is not some elusive enlightenment only Tibetan monks or therapists can access. It's a muscle. You build it by asking hard questions. By surrounding yourself with people who challenge you (not just cheer you). By being brave enough to say, "Maybe I'm wrong." And by being clear on what hill you're willing to die on—and which ones aren't worth the climb.

So whether you're a startup founder trying to punch above your weight, a seasoned executive swimming in molasses meetings, or someone just trying to make sense of your next career move—remember this:

**Know thyself. Always.**

Not the buzzword version. Not the brochure. The real, sometimes messy, brutally honest version. Because that version is the one that wins. That's the one that endures. That's the one who doesn't just survive change—but shapes it.

**Everything else is just noise and flavored sugar water.**

So quit pretending. Quit posturing. And please, for the love of strategy … stop drinking your own damn Kool-Aid.

Self-awareness is the foundation of good strategy. But insight without adaptability is a fancy mirror to shows you what you want to see. And sometimes, the assumptions we cling to are what limit us most.

Let's explore why some dogs shouldn't be in trees.

# key lessons

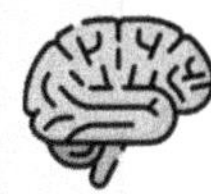

### 1. If You Don't Know Yourself, Your Competitors Will Do It for You.

Most companies "discover themselves" through a crisis they caused.

They chant innovation mantras, set up cornhole sections, and call it culture—while behaving like a bureaucracy in orthopedic shoes.

Self-awareness isn't optional. It's the difference between being **self-correcting** or **market-corrected.**

### 2. Drinking Your Own Kool-Aid Is How Smart People Die Stupid.

Corporate delusion is a full-contact sport:

- Leaders who love buzzwords but hate reality.
- Teams that talk "fail fast" but punish anyone who tries.
- Execs who believe their press releases more than their P&L.

If you can't tell the difference between a vision and hallucination, congratulations—you're the case study everyone warns their interns about.

### 3. Know Your Strengths—or Get Run Over by Someone Who Does.

Being honest about what you're good at isn't touchy-feely. It's survival.

**People without self-awareness** don't climb ladders—they walk into them.

**Companies without self-awareness** don't pivot—they crater. The winners aren't the biggest, loudest, or flashiest ... they're the ones who stop pretending and start acting like who they actually are.

**Self-awareness is the foundation** of good strategy. But insight without adaptability is a fancy mirror to show you what you want to see. And sometimes, the assumptions you cling to are what limit you most.

Let's explore why some dogs shouldn't be in trees.

six

# Dogs Can't Climb Trees ... or Can They?

Experts know 10,000 reasons something won't work.
Beginners only need one reason it might.

We all "know" dogs can't climb trees. Just like we "know" pigs can't fly, square pegs don't fit in round holes, without modifications, and corporate innovation only happens after a QBR and six rounds of approvals ... hah!

But here's the thing: sometimes the most powerful breakthroughs come from not knowing what's *supposed* to be impossible.

I tell my teams: Operate without boundaries. Assume nothing. Question everything. Because once you stop believing in what can't be done, you start discovering what actually *can*.

In the words of Albert Einstein:

**Imagination is more important than knowledge. For knowledge is limited, whereas imagination embraces the entire world, stimulating progress, giving birth to evolution.**

I would listen to Al. He was a smart guy.

Take the story of the dog spotted eight feet up in a tree. Other dogs gather at the bottom, barking and howling in disbelief.

"What the hell are you doing up there? Dogs can't climb trees."

The dog in the tree shrugs, "Nobody told me that."

Boom. That's it. That's the magic.

That dog didn't read the manual. Didn't sit through the training. Didn't wait for permission. He just saw a squirrel—or a challenge—and figured it out. Clawed his way up, one shaky branch at a time.

Now imagine if we all worked like that.

## The Upside of Not Knowing Your Limits

When you don't know your limitations, you're not boxed in by them. You're free to explore, improvise, and push the edges of what's possible. This isn't just motivational poster fluff. This is how real innovation happens!

- Velcro was invented because a guy got curious about burrs stuck to his dog.
- Spanx happened because nobody told Sara Blakely she needed industry experience or an MBA to start a billion-dollar company.
- NASA engineers duct-taped a solution in real time during Apollo 13 because failure wasn't an option—and nobody had time to list all the reasons it wouldn't work.

**The more you know, the more you know what can't be done.**

If any of those people had waited for permission or accepted the "truths" about what they weren't qualified to do, we'd be worse off today.

## The Myth of Expertise

The funny thing about being an "expert"—the more you know, the more you know what can't be done. Expertise is a well-decorated box. Looks nice, feels authoritative. But it's still a box.

Some of the most game changing ideas came from people who weren't credentialed, trained, or remotely qualified on paper. The Wright brothers fixed bicycles. Steve Jobs didn't code. Nobody with a PhD in meteorology suggested building a business around people standing in front of a green screen studio screaming about hurricanes.

The beginners don't see the limitations. They are not bounded by their own experience and biases. They are free to explore the "what if" scenarios. Just like our son, Erik, and his taco tape idea.

And that's where the fun begins.

## When Dumb Questions Are Actually Brilliant

The best strategy sessions I've ever been a part of started with someone asking a question that sounded ridiculous. "What if we could come up with a way of figuring out what our competitors would announce 18-24 months from now?" "What is missing from our product that an ecosystem partner could fulfill for us?" "What if we let customers configure it for themselves?"

How about: "What if I created a thermostat I could configure and manage with my phone app so when we get to our cabin, it's already warm and we're not freezing the first night of arrival?" Tony Fadell is inventor and author of *BUILD: An Unorthodox Guide to Making Things Worth Making*. He came up with that one and it lead to over $300M by the time Nest was acquired by Google for $3.2 Billion.

It's questions and thinking like this that lead to breakthroughs.

## But Wait—Of Course, There's a Catch

Let's be clear: unbounded thinking doesn't mean *reckless* thinking. That dog still had to grip the bark, find the footholds, and figure out how not to fall and break his canine tailbone. The magic only works when ignorance is paired with:

- **Curiosity:** the drive to explore uncharted ground
- **Courage:** the guts to look foolish (or fall out of the metaphorical tree)
- **Support:** a team, environment, or culture that doesn't shoot down the dog just for trying

Without those, "not knowing your limits" just leads to broken bones and bad PowerPoint decks. And scars. Lots of scars.

## Bringing It Home

Next time someone on your team suggests an idea that sounds as absurd as a Beagle in a birch tree, resist the reflective *"that's impossible."* Instead, channel your inner Rufus-the-dog:

1. **Tilt your head and ask:** "What would have to be *true* for this to work?"
2. **Find the lowest branch:** a cheap and cheerful experiment that tests the craziest assumption.
3. **If the branch holds, climb higher.** If it snaps, you've still learned gravity's terms—at minimal cost.

## Your Breakthrough Might Look Ridiculous at First

Here's the truth: Every disruptive idea starts out looking a little stupid. A dog in a tree. A human with a parachute. A garage startup challenging IBM.

And yet ...

Sometimes, that ridiculous leap becomes the next big thing. Sometimes, being the dog who didn't know better is exactly what the world needs.

My advice: stop asking if you can climb the tree. Instead,

**Start asking:**
**What's up there that no one's seen yet?**

Climb that tree and take a look around.

## The Real Problem: The Status Quo

"We've always done it this way." "We tried that once and it didn't work." "Our systems won't allow that."

Excuses, excuses, excuses. **Sigh.**

Seems like we have more excuses for why we can't do thing than why we should try. Artificial boundaries set by people that came before us. Now, I'm not suggesting doing anything illegal, unethical, immoral, or fattening. Just because something didn't work before doesn't mean you can't try a new approach.

**The enemy is the status quo.**

The status quo feels safe. But it's a black hole for innovation. You'll never see the view from the tree if you're not allowed to climb it.

**Status quo:**
**It's where good ideas go to die.**
**Usually in committee.**

## Actionable Insights

Every year, my team picks a few "impossible" projects. It's a part of our continuous improvement process. One was automating win-loss data from our CRM (Customer Relationship Management) system. Another was predicting competitor moves 18-24 months in advance using strategic signals.

Predictably, others in the company labeled these projects as "can't be done."

Both were done. Both delivered major value. And, both started with asking, "why not?"

## Never Negotiate with Someone Who Can't Say "Yes"

I worked for a great CMO who offered me an invaluable piece of advice: "never negotiate with someone who can't say yes."

There are armies of gatekeepers whose job is to say no.

**Find the person who can say yes.**

Sound advice. Really works.

We once shut down a failing product. One angry customer demanded our source code (a.k.a. the family jewels.) For those in tech, you know that's an automatic "NO" to the request. Nobody gets the source code even if we are shutting it down.

Most, actually, nearly all legal people would have flat out refused. But I worked directly with the head of legal, crafted a smart memorandum of understanding (MOU) with very restrictive and specific conditions, and this was delivered to the angry customer.

We called their bluff.

**It would never have made it to that point if I didn't work with the guy who could say yes.**

Turns out, once they saw what it would cost to build a development team, they backed off from their demand. Their revelation: they realized they had no idea how to run a software business.

We tore up the agreement and worked to find them an alternative solution. Win-win. But it would never have made it to that point if I didn't work with the guy who could say yes.

This worked because I had:

- A vision.
- The imagination to explore alternatives.
- The ability to execute.

And that, my friend, is where we go next.

# key lessons

**1. Limits Are Mostly Made Up—Usually by People Who've Stopped Trying.**

"Dogs can't climb trees."

Sure—if you're the kind of dog who needs a committee, a pilot program, and an approved budget to chase a squirrel.

Innovation doesn't come from the experts; it comes from the clueless optimist who didn't know the rules and therefore didn't follow them.

The world isn't held back by ignorance—it's held back by people who think they're too smart to try.

**2. The Status Quo Isn't Safe—It's Where Great Ideas Go to Die.**

If your company's favorite phrase is "we've always done it this way," congratulations. You're working in an innovation hospice.

Nothing kills progress faster than people defending outdated systems, old scars, and mediocre past decisions.

The status quo feels comfortable right up until someone else eats your lunch and leaves you holding the bill.

**3. Imagination Beats Expertise—Especially When the Experts Are the Problem.**

Experts know 10,000 reasons something won't work. Beginners only need one reason it might.

And somehow, the beginners keep inventing the future while the experts keep writing PowerPoints about "risk mitigation."

You want breakthroughs? Ask the dumb question. Try the dumb idea. Ignore the dumb rules. Everything "impossible" was invented by someone who didn't know better—or didn't care.

part two

# Vision, Imagination, and Execution

## Author's Note

# Vision, Imagination, and Execution

Have you ever wondered why so many strategies look brilliant in a slide deck but fall apart in the real world? Or why the spark of a great idea often fizzles before it ever sees daylight? Or why execution, no matter how much effort you pour in, can still feel like spinning wheels in the mud?

That's the challenge of turning vision into reality. Vision alone isn't enough. Without additional elements, it's just a daydream. Imagination without grounding can send you racing down blind alleys. Execution without clarity burns resources but doesn't move the ball forward. And when organizations cling to the loudest customer or the highest-paid person in the room, they mistake activity for strategy. They begins to forget why they started in the first place: to serve a market.

But when vision, imagination, observation, and execution link together, they become a loop that bends markets. This is where sparks catch fire. Ideas born in odd places ... like a kid's invention of "taco tape" to fix a collapsing taco shell. Ideas turn into strategies that shift industries. This is where observation cuts through blind spots and corporate antibodies, and execution stops being firefighting and starts being deliberate, disciplined action.

In the chapters ahead, you'll see how to recognize patterns early, frame a future others can't yet see, and protect imagination from the gravitational pull of the status quo. You'll learn how to test assumptions, pressure-test plans before the market does it for you, and survive the messy middle where optimism collides with deadlines. You'll see that tools like pre-mortems, red teaming, and war games aren't academic—they're survival gear.

If Part One was about becoming strategic, Part Two is about staying strategic when the game turns hard because every vision eventually collides with reality—in the market, in the boardroom, or in the middle of a product launch. The question isn't whether your strategy will get hit. It will. The question is whether you've built the loop strong enough to bend without breaking.

seven

# The Vision Game ... from Bar Chess to Market Moves

When you treat your ideas like they matter—
when you sell the story—people start leaning in.

The most strategic game I ever played didn't happen in a boardroom. It happened at a bar. No board. No rules. Just two guys, a table full of condiments, and enough beer to believe a mustard bottle could lead a surprise flank attack on the pepper shaker. We called it Bar Chess.

My boss, Greg, and I would usually start playing after our second adult beverage was delivered. There were no instructions—just improv. He'd move the salt shaker two inches to the left. I'd counter with a Sweet'n Low blockade. Greg might sacrifice the Tabasco bottle in a fake out and then swoop in with a devastating shot glass strike. The goal? Win the game that didn't exist—*and look deadly serious doing it.*

We never explained it to anyone. That was part of the charm. But inevitably, people would gather, watching like it was Kasparov vs. Deep Blue. Because when you treat your ideas like they matter —when you *sell* the story—people start leaning in. They want to know what they're missing.

## Vision vs. Ideation—Bar Chess Edition

Vision—it's not some buzzword reserved for TED Talks and executive offsites. It *is* the ability to look at a cluttered mess of condiments on a sticky bar table and *see* the potential for a coordinated offensive. It's that flicker of strategic foresight that says, "If I nudge the mustard here and the Tabasco doesn't flinch, I've got a shot at controlling the ketchup."

That's vision: sensing patterns before they form. Reading the room. Anticipating the market. Plotting two moves ahead while everyone else is still wiping beer off their sleeves.

Ideation, on the other hand, is what happens after that spark. It's the creative scrimmage of exploring how to turn that vision into action. Do you fake left with the salt shaker? Block the straw dispenser? Use the coffee cream milkette as bait? There's no single playbook—just a flurry of wild, half-brilliant possibilities.

In short …

**Vision is the aha! moment–**
**where you see where this could go.**

**Ideation is the now what?–**
**how you might actually get there.**

## Vision and Tacos: Where Ideas Really Come From

Ideation. The art of getting an idea from nowhere. Sometimes it feels mystical. Other times, it shows up at the dinner table—usually when you're not looking for it.

Take our youngest son, Erik. He was in junior high school, sitting at the table eating tacos when the shell started falling apart mid-bite. He looked down and said with total seriousness:

**"I think I should invent taco tape."**

Something to hold the taco together so it doesn't self-destruct before you're halfway through.

Vision and ideation born in the same bite. And get this: a few years later, someone did invent a taco tape-like product, not Erik, unfortunately.

That's the thing about these ideas. They don't always come around when summoned. They sneak up on you. In the car. On a hike. Watching TV. Sitting on an airplane. Or chewing on dinner. And while you can't always control when they arrive, you can control whether you pay attention when they do.

We're all born with this spark. Some call it creativity. I like to call it **strategic imagination**—the ability to see something that isn't there yet and give it shape. Some people seem to access it on demand and more importantly, they know how to act on it. Dr. Lydia Kostopolous talks about our imagination deficiency in her book, *Imagination Dilemma.*

When ideation—that inspiration, that insight, that brainstorm —becomes a plan, that's called a strategy.

## Seeing, Testing, and Adjusting

In business, everyone wants to know your vision. Investors. Analysts. Customers. And yes, your team. So here's mine from one of the gnarliest strategic rebuilds I ever led.

We had an aging product, an angry customer base, and a product that had just been acquired from a money-losing competitor. Add to that: an OEM deal reversal—one where we developed software for another company, only to buy it back after they realized selling application software to enterprises wasn't in their DNA.

These customers represented the largest enterprises in the world across finance, manufacturing, telco, supply chain, etc.

Most would have called it a mess. I saw it as a launchpad. Talk about strategic improv.

**The Vision.** Build a platform that helped customers learn, test, and confidently deploy new mission-critical software into production—with fewer headaches and far more control.

**The Strategy.** Combine the strengths of three product lines—our product, the OEM rescue, and the acquired one—into a single "best-of-breed" solution in 18 months. I started with the desired press release I wanted to issue at the end and then reverse-engineered the rest.

**The Problem.** We had backlash. Loud, public backlash. Analysts torched us in reports before even learning about our plans. Customers were threatening lawsuits. Some cried "monopoly," while others just wanted their money back.

**Vision gets you leaning forward.**

Not a whole lot of fun, actually none at all.

**But the noise hid the signal**—customers weren't necessarily mad because of what we were doing. They were mad because we didn't show them the **value.**

The solution? Expand the strategy playbook.

I created a Customer Advisory Board with users from all three products. Brought in third-party experts, industry luminaries, and trusted consultants who became our collaborators to help customers. Commissioned training guides from third-party companies who became partners in the venture. Started building what today we'd call an **ecosystem.** Back then, people thought vendors were supposed to go it alone. We didn't. Win-win for everyone in the ecosystem and especially our customers.

Then I hit the road. Not to sell, but to show. To demo. To listen. To rebuild trust one flight, one prototype review, and one conversation at a time. We only lost two customers during that entire transformation—which, honestly, felt like winning the Super Bowl.

**Vision is where you're headed.**

**Strategy is how you make people want to go there with you.**

And if you want to earn their trust? Show up. Listen. Show them their future. Show you care.

## When Vision Becomes Outdated and Irrelevant

I once worked for a company with an Olympic-level talent for denial. Their strategy? Go full Ostrich mode: head in the sand, eyes closed, ears off, and totally blind to what was coming.

They sold expensive, proprietary systems while the market was shifting towards cheaper, commodity-based platforms. Instead of adapting, they clung to the belief that customers would stay loyal—despite mounting data to the contrary. Spoiler alert: they didn't adapt like Star Trek's Borg to attacks.

Quarterly analysis showed we would miss revenue target by a wide swing. I won't say how much but it would be painfully obvious to everyone—especially the markets. Quarter-after-quarter the data showed huge swing-and-a-miss but management didn't want to believe the data.

This was textbook denial.

Their messaging? A confused mess. The strategy? A shrug. No one could explain why spending more on our high-cost solution made sense, and customers began to walk. The numbers clearly showed a steep decline, but nobody wanted to believe it was happening. Eventually, leadership pivoted to embrace commodity platforms—but by then, it was too late. Game over.

This wasn't a single-point failure. It was death by a thousand bad decisions: overconfidence bias on full display, groupthink, and execs trapped in their own echo chamber.

**What if someone solves this problem a completely different way?**

Moral of the story? Keep your head up. The market doesn't care how good your past was. It cares if you're going to still be relevant tomorrow.

Ostriches don't win markets—
they just get run over.

## The Strategy Loop: A Playbook You Can Use

I've always liked frameworks that sound deceptively simple. Here's mine:

**Strategy = Vision x Imagination x Observation x Action**

Four variables. All are interdependent. If anyone is zero, your strategy flops.

Let's unpack it.

### Vision: What problem are you really solving?

This is your North Star. It needs to be crisp, clear, and repeatable without PowerPoint. If your elevator pitch turns into a TED Talk, you're not ready.

Think Tony Fadell. His vision for the Nest thermostat? *Control your home's temperature from anywhere using your phone.* That's it. No jargon. No complexity. Just pure, clean value.

Now add this: How is your solution different? Not "better"—different. Because first-mover advantage is like milk on a hot day—it spoils fast. If your idea can't evolve, competitors will catch up or eat your lunch, sometimes both.

### Imagination: How else could this be solved?

This is where the magic happens—and where most teams short-circuit. Andy Grove of Intel used to obsess over this: "What if someone solves this problem a completely different way?"

That's the question.

Don't just think outside the box. Throw the box out. How would Tesla solve this? How would Pixar? How would a team of 5th graders armed with glue sticks and caffeine handle it?

Channel your inner Einstein: "Imagination is more important than knowledge."

### Observation: What's really going on in the market?

Be honest. Brutally so. What's the market saying—not what you *want* it to say?

**I call it sanity insurance.**

Too often, we fall in love with our idea and skip validation. That's a fantasy, not strategy.

Talk to users. Study competitors. Watch where people hesitate, complain, or pay extra. That's signal.

### Action: How do you test, break, and rebuild before it's too late?

This is where vision becomes reality. The trick? Move fast, test early, and invite failure. Yes, invite it.

One of my go-to tools is the **pre-mortem.** Think post-mortem, but in reverse.

Get your team in a room and say: "It's a year from now. Our product tanked. Everyone's mad. What went wrong?" Then shut up and let the chaos pour out.

Some call this **red teaming**—having someone play the antagonist. I call it sanity insurance.

Want to level up? Try a full-on business war game. Role-play your competitors—LARPing (Live Action Role Playing). Simulate customer objections. Pressure-test your plan before the real bullets fly.

# key lessons

## 1. Vision Isn't Magic—It's Seeing the Game Before Anyone Admits a Game Exists.

Real vision isn't a TED Talk slide. It's looking at a sticky bar table full of ketchup and Splenda and spotting a strategy no one else sees.

Most leaders can't see two inches past the PowerPoint deck; true visionaries can spot market moves using **condiments and beer.**

If you can't do that? You're not "visionary." You're just loud.

## 2. Taco Tape Proves the Average Teenager Is Smarter Than Most Innovation Committees.

Our kid invented taco tape out of pure frustration during dinner.

Corporate innovation teams would have needed:

- Six quarters
- Three Analyst Firm consultations
- A $500k "Design Thinking Offsite"
- And 9 VPs to approve the font

  ...before concluding "there is no viable market for taco adhesion solutions."

Stop pretending bureaucracy breeds brilliance. It barely breeds functioning printers.

*(continued)*

# key lessons

**3. Denial Is the #1 Cause of Corporate Death.**
Some companies cling to outdated strategies like they're trying to win a hide-and-seek game against reality.

The data is screaming "WE ARE DYING," and leadership is like: "No we're not—the customers are just confused!"

Yeah. Confused about why you're still in business. By the time your exec team finally pulls its head out of the sand, the competition has:

- Stolen your customers.
- Stolen your market.
- Stolen your lunch.
- And probably stolen your parking spot too.

***Try this:*** *Grab a napkin. No, really. Draw the landscape of your product, service, or idea like it's bar chess. Who's the salt shaker? Who's the ketchup? What's your opening move? How will the Tabasco retaliate?*

Vision gets you leaning forward. But nothing kills vision faster than cozy habits and internal politics.

Before we dream bigger, let's talk about the corporate antibodies that show up the second you try.

eight

# Innovation, Status Quo, Blind Spots, and Market Myopia

Always build for the market, not just one client.

Greg used to say, "At some point size becomes the enemy to innovation." Why do some companies continue to break through repeatedly while others cling to a failing status quo?

I've worked across the tech spectrum and one thing's clear: size doesn't guarantee smart.

As a product manager, I've turned around failing product lines, rebooted products bleeding cash, and launched new products into 50-year-old mature markets where we knocked out long-time incumbents who felt a sense of entitlement. That kind of win takes serious innovation—sometimes more than launching something fresh at a startup with nothing to lose.

Repeatedly I've seen this one pattern: big companies slowly drift to an inward focus. They stop listening to the market and start chasing the loudest customer and their demands. Or start focusing on internal agendas without regard to what the market wants, despite losing market share quarter-over-quarter. That's how strategy dies—one custom feature at a time.

Take a startup I'm an advisor for in Canada. They had a major marquee customer waving a list of feature demands. The cofounder CEO asked me what to do. My answer: **build for the market, not just one client.** That advice still holds.

I've fought my entire career to keep product strategy aligned with what the broader market needs—not just what the biggest customer wants today. That's the difference between scaling and stalling.

## The Curse of the Innovator's Dilemma

Clayton Christensen nailed it within the pages of *The Innovator's Dilemma: When New Technologies Cause Great Firms to Fail*:

> Companies get so focused on their biggest customers they lose sight of the real prize: the market.

I've seen it too many times. Product teams bend over backwards for a "strategic" customer. Sometimes it's to keep the customer happy. Sometimes it's to avoid a churn threat. Either way, it's a distraction.

I'm not saying ignore big customers. I'm saying **put their asks in the proper context.** One custom request that costs you the bandwidth to deliver something impactful to 100 others is a terrible trade if you've got real competition breathing down your neck.

I've often found that a "special feature" request is not applicable to most of the customer base. When that happens, I will give the customer a specific price quote for their request based on time and materials—their reaction tells me all I need to know. Or I tell them: find 25 other customers that want the same feature. If you can, we'll talk. I'm not giving anything away for free that might prevent further market capture. Unless you're a custom job-shop, resist the temptation to do one-offs.

The bigger you get, the more you forget how to play offense. You start building for comfort instead of conquest.

**Greg was right:
size becomes the enemy when you
stop hunting and start babysitting.**

## Corporate Antibodies at Work ... and Tactics to Counter Them

Corporate antibodies are those lovely folks who show up the second you try and innovate: ready to block, stall, or quietly—sometimes not so quietly—kill anything that threatens their routine. Their job? Defend the status quo like it's a national treasure.

And the thing about status quos? They're contagious. Like a virus with good PR, they replicate fast, protect outdated processes, and punch like Bruce Lee unless someone steps in and says, "not anymore."

**People fear loss more than they value gain.**

When you want to challenge the status quo, you've got two framing options: **negative** and **positive.** Both work, but you've got to know which lever to pull.

### Negative Framing: Triggering Action ... But Just Barely

Example of a negative frame might be: "Our flagship product is slipping fast—from #2 to #5 in market usage. If we don't move now, we're going to lose relevance, and the competition's already in our customers' inboxes."

Why this works:

- It emphasizes loss
- It creates urgency
- It highlights momentum *against* you

Executives often respond—*but just enough to put out the fire.* They'll patch the hole, not rethink the ship. That is status quo bias at work.

Daniel Kahneman and Amos Tversky's *Prospect Theory* explains it: people fear loss more than they value gain. So they'll act, but usually only to restore the old normal, not create a new one.

### Positive Framing: Breaking the Mold

To really shake loose the status quo, you need a positive frame that **makes the current state feel small**—but without making the exec feel dumb for supporting it.

Try something like:

> "What got us here was great. But we're in a new game now—and we need a new playbook. Our competitors are already moving, but if we get this right, we don't just catch up—we leapfrog."

You're not selling upside alone—you're reframing the present as **incomplete.** That's the key.

### Even Apple Has Antibodies

Tony Fadell thought building the iPod would be a dream gig at Apple. Turns out, corporate antibodies swarmed. People protected turf, stalled progress, and resisted change.

It wasn't until Steve Jobs made it crystal clear—**help Tony or start job hunting**—that things finally started to move.

Nobody is immune. Not even Apple.

**If the antibodies don't kill you, the animal kingdom might.**

## Dangerous Animals to Watch For

As companies grow and gain customers, they often shift from market focus to customer appeasement. And when that happens, the zoo opens.

Team Productboard's goal is to help companies build truly excellent products. Creating *The Dangerous Animals Handler's Toolbox, its nailed many "animals" that can sabotage a company.*

A few classics you'll recognize:

- **RHiNO:** *Really High-value New Opportunity*
  Obsessive about closing one deal with one-off features. Sounds strategic—kills your roadmap.
- **HiPPO:** *Highest Paid Person's Opinion*
  No data. Just power. Wants a pet feature pushed to the top because … title.
- **GOOSE:** *Guesstimating Overly Optimistic Scheduling Estimates*
  Pulls deadlines out of thin air. Doesn't understand development cycles. Result: blown timelines, disappointed customers, missed revenue.

These creatures may look harmless. They're not. Each one derails product strategy and drags you away from serving the market. And there are more animal species to be avoid. I've only listed three of them.

## Marketing Myopia … Still Alive and Kicking

In the July-August 1960 *HBR* publication, Harvard's Theodore Levitt warned us (I've added the bold emphasis):

> Companies in the grip of **marketing myopia** are blinded by the products they make and are **unable** to see the larger purpose or true market dynamics.
>
> These companies spend **billions** of dollars making their new generation of products **just slightly better** than their old generation of product.
>
> They use entirely **internal** measures of progress and success—patents, technical achievements, and the like—without stepping back to consider the **needs of consumers and the changing marketplace.**

That's why version 2.0 is often just version 1.4 in new packaging. And that's when competitors start kicking up dust and leaving you behind.

**Blind spots aren't caused by lack of data.**

Classic case: Railroads didn't decline because people stopped needing transportation. They failed because they thought they were in the **railroad** business, not the **transportation** business.

"People don't want a quarter-inch drill bit. They want a quarter-inch hole." Stay focused on customer outcomes, not your internal trophies.

## Blind Spots: The Ones That Kill

Levitt exposed the disease. Dr. Benjamin Gilad put a name to the symptoms: **strategic blind spots** in his book, *Opposite of Noise: The Power of Competitive Intelligence.*

Blind spots aren't caused by lack of data. They're caused by:

- Biases
- Assumptions
- Mental models that no longer apply, but no one wants to let go of

**"The most dangerous blind spots are those leaders defend with pride."**

Here are a few of Gilad's greatest hits:

1. **Success Blindness:** Past wins = false invincibility
2. **Confirmation Bias:** Cherry-picking feel = good data you want
3. **Groupthink:** No dissent = no defense
4. **Competitor Dismissal:** Ignoring the ankle biters
5. **Data Overload:** Dashboards ≠ insights

The kicker? The threat isn't the competitor … it's **your inability to see them clearly** or **take them seriously.**

## How to Kill Blind Spots Before They Kill You

Gilad doesn't just diagnose, he prescribes:

**Blind spots aren't mistakes.**

- **Build a culture of intelligence:** Where questions beat assumptions.
- **Institutionalize war games and red teaming:** Simulate the worst-case senario. Stress-test the sacred cows.
- **Make competitive intelligence strategic:** Not buried in market research reports.
- **Hire iconoclasts:** People who challenge the obvious and ask, "What if?"

In the end, it's not the market that kills you—it's the blind spots you choose to ignore. That's handing your market to the competition on a silver platter.

### Exploiting Your Competitor's Blind Spots

Blind spots can kill you, but they can also be weapons if you know how to use them. I've used them to take down competitors several times.

The easiest target? Overconfidence. Success blindness. Competitors are so sure of themselves that arrogance drips from every sales pitch. You'd think they solved world hunger when they can't even solve their own churn problem.

When you spot one, don't just counter … make them prove their claims:

- "What data backs that claim?"
- "Can any customer confirm it using standard products?"
- "How were results generated?"
- "Will you indemnify my business if you're wrong?"
- "Guarantee it in writing?"

Half the time, you won't even have to attack. You just need to show the customer how to ask the right questions. The cracks appear on their own.

### The CFO Is Your Ally

When the tech team's in love with the wrong product, fighting them head-on is usually a losing battle. Go find the CFO.

**Organizations don't fix blind spots. People do.**

A good CFO lives in the work of risk versus return.

- **Due diligence:** Big purchases need solid business cases.
- **Risk mitigation:** Understand the risks and have a Plan B.
- **Vendor stability:** Can they deliver, comply and survive.
- **Strategic fit:** Does it align with goals, CapEx, and cash flow?

I remember one of our teams losing a deal, and I asked for a meeting with the customer's CFO—not to reverse the decision, but to have a business conversation.

I laid out the numbers: in the competitor's own public filings, less than **3.8%** of their revenue was reinvested into this "strategic" product the tech team wanted. The product generated **0.065%** of total company revenue. Our investment and commitment dwarfed theirs.

The CFO laughed and said, "Thanks for keeping this fact-based. We won't be buying that product."

We had their purchase order the following week.

**Organizations don't fix blind spots. People do. And it takes a spine.**

If you want to break the status quo, you have to see clearly—and keep seeing clearly when it is inconvenient.

# key lessons

### 1. Innovation Dies When Companies Start Believing Their Own Marketing.

The fastest way to become irrelevant is to confuse "big customer requests" with "market direction."

If your strategy is built around appeasing one squeaky wheel, congratulations—you're not innovating, you're babysitting.

### 2. Corporate Antibodies Are Just Bureaucrats with Better Titles.

Innovation blockers show up fast:

"Can't do that."

"Not on the roadmap."

"Needs alignment."

Translation: they like the status quo because it keeps them employed.

### 3. Blind Spots Don't Just Cost You Deals—They Cost You the Future.

The moment a leader starts ignoring data because it "doesn't align with their gut," the death clock starts.

Blind spots aren't mistakes. They're **self-inflicted strategic lobotomies.**

If you want to break the status quo, you have to see clearly—and keep seeing clearly when it is inconvenient.

nine

# The Courage to See Clearly

Short-sighted thinking isn't just annoying ... it's dangerous.

Midway through my career, I worked for a guy whose cowlicks could've made Sonic the Hedgehog jealous. Hair like a wind tunnel. Ego like a black hole.

He was the "smartest guy in the room," just ask him. He didn't care about my $500M Annual Recurring Revenue (ARR) business segment. He was an "ideas guy," too busy chasing shiny objects to notice what was already working.

In one business review, he **demanded** I eliminate the largest single chunk of my portfolio, roughly $180M in recurring revenue. His reason? "It's just a drop in the bucket. I need for you to *think bigger.*"

I reminded Mr. Big Ideas that $180M, while small in percentage terms, was still **real money.** As a publicly held company, someone, like a shareholder, might want to know what happened. His response? A shrug. Zero concern for the financial dominos it would tip. Or shareholder value. Turned "executive responsibility" into an oxymoron.

So I ran through the possibilities:

1. He didn't understand how this segment facilitated other company revenue.
2. He was setting me up to fail: cut revenue, then blame me for the decline.
3. He was a Dunning-Kruger case: loud, confident, and clueless.
4. Or maybe the segment just wasn't shiny enough for his attention span.

Most likely, all the above.

I documented my concerns in an email, laid out the shareholder risk, and asked for finance to validate any plan to cut that revenue. He never replied.

Months later, Mr. Big Ideas proudly announced his pet project had pulled in $6M in six months. He called it a success. I called it something unprintable.

**It's not just top-down blindness.**

I did the math: $6M vs. $180M.

'Nuff said.

This type of short-sighted thinking isn't just annoying … it's dangerous. Strategic bias doesn't always show up wearing a name tag. Sometimes, it's disguised as innovation, ambition, or that ever-popular phrase: "we need to think bigger." But chasing big ideas without understanding the foundation is how companies collapse under their own hype when Ignoring boring-but-reliable revenue.

That's not strategy.

That's self-sabotage dressed in buzzwords.

Here's the lesson: when faced with leadership that treats real business like a hobby project, you've got three choices: **conform,**

**fight,** or **walk.** I chose to fight. Because walking away from something that would have damaged my credibility wasn't an option.

Cutting something because it isn't flashy is how businesses trip over their own shoelaces. Before we chase those big ideas, we need to respect the "boring" lines holding the company up. Ignore them, and the foundation cracks.

Strategic clarity doesn't just come from spreadsheets or market trend lines. Sometimes, it comes from the courage to challenge assumptions, especially when they belong to someone higher on the org chart. And that's when things get tricky.

But here's the real kicker: it's not just top-down blindness. Strategic failure often starts at the micro level … when smart people stop asking questions, stop checking assumptions, and stop looking beyond what they want to believe. That blindness isn't always malicious. Sometimes, it's just human.

And that sets the stage to the most dangerous kind of blindness: the kind you don't even know you have. The one that shows up in meetings when someone says, "I don't agree with your conclusion." That moment when logic collides with perception, and you realize … maybe they don't see what you see.

## Do You See What I See?

Every product manager … hell, every professional eventually hears the phrase:

**"I don't agree with your conclusion."**

Doesn't matter if it's from an engineer, a VP, or someone whose credential is speaking loudly in your meetings. Your gut tightens. Heart rate spikes. Cue up Kahneman's System Two: you've just gone from calm to combat.

In my experience, this moment boils down to one thing:

**They don't have the data you do.**

Not because they're dumb or difficult (well, sometimes), but because they literally can't see what you see.

### The Fix: Show Them the Data

Lay out your assumptions. Walk them through the logic. Nine times out of ten, they'll arrive at the same place you did if your analysis is solid and your reasoning is sound.

And if they challenge an assumption? Great. Listen. If it's valid, rerun the model. Most of the time, that one variable won't change the outcome, but the fact you listened earns credibility and shows you're not married to your ego.

## When Smart People Miss the Point

Some execs don't lack IQ, they lack the curiosity to see outside their own mental models. That's not stupidity. That's strategy-blindness. It's what happens when your title outruns your learning curve.

### Biases, the Mandella Effect, and the Status Quo Trap

Biases are the silent saboteurs of strategic thinking. And, when paired with the status quo, that's a recipe for corporate strangulation.

The status quo bias keeps people clinging to what's familiar—even when it's failing. But that's just one shade of the problem. Here are a few more culprits that distort decision making:

**1. Confirmation Bias**

Cling to the good news; ignore the churn.

**"Our customers love our product." Meanwhile, your market share's ghosting you.**

2. **Authority Bias**

   You defer to leaders—not because they're right, but because they're in charge. Title trumps truth.

3. **Sunk Cost Fallacy**

   Throwing good money, and time, and people after bad. "We've invested too much to stop now." The fast way to budget hell.

4. **Over-Confidence Bias**

   Past wins become a false predictor of future success. At the org level, it's arrogance. At the personal level, it's the Dunning-Kruger effect: loud, proud, and clueless.

And then there's the **Mandella Effect,** a collective false memory. When an entire group swears something is true, even though it isn't. For example:

- "Luke, I am your father" actually, it's "No, I am your father."
- The Monopoly Man? No monocle. Never had one … that's Mr. Peanut.
- Your bologna is from "Oscar Mayer," not "Meyer."
- Fruit of the Loom logo? No cornucopia.

We remember wrong. We trust our memory too much. And we assume others are right because they remember it wrong with us.

That's the danger. These blind spots and illusions can steer entire teams, companies, even industries, off course. As Jack Reacher, author Lee Child's nomadic protagonist of his popular thriller book series says:

**"Assumptions kill."<br>In business, they don't just kill ideas.<br>They kill careers, strategies,<br>and whole markets.**

## When It's Not About Data—It's About Opinion

Ben Gilad gave me life-changing advice I still use:

**Never answer with "in my opinion"**

Why? Because the second you say, "in my opinion," you've opened the door for someone to debate you. That's not your analysis debated, it is **you.** Your opinion becomes the battleground.

**Strategic blindness isn't about stupidity.**

Let's say someone asks,

**What do you think Competitor X will do if we launch Y?**

Don't answer with "I think ..." Instead say:

**Competitor X will likely respond by doing Z.**

Now the argument shifts from being about your **opinion** to being about the **competitor's behavior,** which is the actual subject, and something you've studied. You've reframed the conversation from personal to professional.

Trust me here: this one technique saved me a **lot of bloodshed, specifically, my own.**

But not all disagreements are about data or opinion. Sometimes, the real problem is what people don't see. Strategic blindness isn't about stupidity. Instead, it's about assumption, ego, and a dangerous confidence that the future will look like the past.

## Making the Invisible Obvious

"Seeing around corners" isn't magic—it's a mix of foresight, pattern recognition, anticipation, and gut feel. It's what happens when vision meets curiosity and experience. Startups love to flaunt it. But even the most boring, legacy-laden industries need it—maybe more than anyone. Because even in mature markets, the right kind of insight can turn the obvious into opportunity before the rest of the world sees it coming.

My product gig: crack a 50-year-old market and figure out how to become the leader. Two legacy giants owned the space, trading customers like baseball cards. Classic Porter-style "good" competition—stable, predictable, and polite. Everyone played by the rules. No blood, just business.

Until I came along.

My product was 3x more expensive than the legacy buys … but also 98% faster. And here's the kicker: customers didn't need to change a thing. Same workflows and processes. Zero change. No retraining. Just plug in and go faster.

We upended competitors' entire business model, and they knew it. That's why they scoffed. They dismissed it, trashed it, spun their own "alternative facts." Classic denial. They wouldn't respond until it was too late—when we'd already taken the market and left them to fast-follow our innovation. Textbook Levitt's Marketing Myopia.

So we built a plan.

We found early adopters who were desperate to break out of the status quo. We worked with industry analysts who could champion our approach without openly slamming the incumbents. And we made damn sure customers had compelling, measurable reasons to justify paying 3x more.

## Same Workflow. Way More Profit.

We zeroed in on two reasons customers would gladly pay a premium for our product—even though it did the same things as the legacy stuff, just 98% faster.

**Make more money. Or save more money.** That was the pitch. Direct and simple.

We didn't get bogged down in speeds, feeds, or tech specs. We focused on outcomes and appealed to the emotional benefits of our product. Because no matter what the industry, every customer understands two things: profit and efficiency. Lead with those value propositions and they'll listen.

## Outrun, Outgun, Outdone

Just as we expected, the competitors trashed our launch. It didn't matter.

Customer outcomes spoke louder than their noise—and we armed our sales teams with case study proof examples:

### Make More Money

67% more daily orders, $80M additional revenue over 5 years, 2,000% ROI.

### Save More Money

$10M in cost savings over 5 years, 99% space reclaimed, no new infrastructure needed for legacy expansion.

And here's the kicker: no changes to the customer operations. Complete transparency with great outcomes.

Competitors scrambled to copy us, but by the time they caught their breath, three years later, we had already taken the crown. One even threw in the towel and exited the market completely.

This wasn't just a strategy win … it was a $1B+ war chest that funded other projects.

## Vision Isn't Enough … You Need Guts to Defend It

Vision without guts is just a mood board.

Because the biggest blind spot? It's not the market.

It's in the mirror.

In the end, beauty may be in the eye of the beholder—but blind spots live there too.

The leaders who win? They question what they see, challenge what they think they know … and still have the guts to bet big when it counts.

Clarity without motion is a TED Talk. The next step is messy, practical, unglamorous: disciplined execution. Here's how teams actually move.

# key lessons

### 1. The Most Dangerous People in Business Are the Ones Who Think Big and See Nothing.

If you want a masterclass in strategic blindness, just watch an executive try to kill $180M because it's "not exciting."

This isn't vision.

It's ego-driven self-sabotage.

### 2. Disagreement Isn't a Challenge—It's a Diagnostic Tool.

If some people "don't agree," it's usually because they're operating with the data equivalent of dial-up internet access (think AOL).

They probably didn't get the "You've Got Mail" message. Give them the facts.

If they still resist, congratulations—you've found egos dressed as insight.

### 3. Blind Spots Don't Just Hurt Strategy—They Create Corporate Crime Scenes.

Bias + arrogance + assumptions = organizational Darwinism.

But assumptions don't age like wine. They age like mayonnaise.

And they rot everything around them.

**The next step is messy, practical, unglamorous: disciplined execution. Here's how teams actually move.**

ten

# The Discipline of Execution

Execution is what separates
the visionaries from the one-hit wonders.

Right out of college, I had a shot to join a startup. As a beta tester, I knew they had something special—a killer app. But they couldn't offer much: no relocation, no salary to speak of. Just some founder's stock. I passed. That little startup? They were Lotus ... as in Lotus 1-2-3 ... the application that lit the fuse on the IBM PC revolution.

I didn't know what *founder's stock* was. Or what missing out on it would feel like. Spoiler alert: it stings.

Startups lure you in with the dream: get rich, retire early, brag forever. But here's the reality check—10% flame out in year one. By year ten, 90% are toast according to CB Insights, a research group that tracks and compares the world's companies. Vegas might give you better odds.

The real magic? It's not getting lucky once. It's the ones who pull it off repeatedly that I pay attention to. They've got more than a flashy pitch or good timing. They've got execution.

I've been part of some startups. And I've watched them fail. Same with big companies. The common thread? Not the idea. Not the funding. Not even the team. It's the execution.

Execution is what separates the visionaries from the one-hit wonders. And it's not just a startup problem. It's an *everybody* problem.

## When the Firefighter Is Also the Arsonist

### A Lesson on Implosion

One startup I joined had all the hallmarks of a breakout success: breakthrough tech, a proven manufacturing partner, award-winning design, and a veteran team with wins under its belt. Hardware and software were humming. VCs were happy, a rarity. I was leading product management: collateral, pricing, competitive positioning —check, check, and check.

Then came the chaos agent.

One of the founders brought in a person with a strong personality and stronger political agenda. Within months, the team started fracturing. Backchannel whispering. Team members pitted against one another. Finger pointing at who was to blame for delays that were increasingly creating tension. It spread like a virus, and productivity fell off a cliff.

Still, we pulled off a killer product launch. But behind the curtain, another disaster loomed. The CFO failed to hedge against currency swings. When the dollar crashed, our costs skyrocketed. We were locked into a contract that made every shipment a loss. We might as well have shipped cash in every box.

In months, the cash was gone. Layoffs. Founders forced out. Morale in the basement.

Even after winning Product of the Year, the company collapsed—undone by toxic culture and bad financial management.

**Lesson learned:** Never hire someone who wants to play both firefighter and arsonist—with your company as the prize.

## A Solution in Search of a Problem

### A Lesson in "Yes, It Can Do That Too"

Flashback to 1999—VC deals were being inked on the back of napkins at Sullivan's Steakhouse in Austin. Money was flowing like the rivers into Lake Travis.

**Scope creep exploded. Progress stalled and slowed.**

A CEO friend pulled me into a startup spun out of academia. The tech? Technology with a rollback mechanism for database production environments that hit the wall due to problems with upgrades.

We validated the idea. Customers wanted it. They'd pay for it. We had a focused use case.

Then the trouble started.

The researchers-turned-developers began chasing shiny ideas. "It could do this … and that … and maybe solve climate change too!" Scope creep exploded. Progress slowed and then stalled.

Meanwhile, our angel investors—zero tech chops—grew restless. They didn't understand why the magic wasn't happening faster. Impatience met inexperience. That mix is nitroglycerin.

Eventually, our head of development—a real engineer—quit. The angels pulled the plug and torched the house.

**Lessons learned:**

1. Don't take money from people who don't understand the game.

2. Don't confuse academic theory with working code.
3. Focus solves problems—distractions create them.

## Equal Opportunity Failure

Execution failures aren't just a startup problem—they're universal. Big companies, small ones, public or private, it doesn't matter. I've talked with folks at industry conferences from every corner of tech and strategy, and they all echo the same frustration: the vision is there, but execution keeps tanking it. Late to the market. Lacking competitive features. No sense of urgency.

Execution failure is the great equalizer. It doesn't care if you're Kodak, Nokia, Blackberry, or Michelin's PAX. Others just fizzle out quietly behind closed doors. Even within companies, I've seen projects launch like rockets only to nosedive and crater halfway through. It's not just what you're building—it's how you build it.

## Execution Is a Lot Like Cooking

Here's how I think about it: execution is like cooking. Strategy is no different than a great meal—the magic isn't in the recipe. It's in the execution.

**When execution works, it's magic.**

As a semi-decent amateur chef and competitive BBQ enthusiast, I've served up meals that people still talk about—and some wish they could forget. The difference? Ingredients.

- Wrong ingredients
- Bad substitutions
- Too much of something that should have been subtle

Same deal with execution. You need the right team with the right skills, the right tools, the right environment—and the right amount of heat.

No shortcuts. No ketchup masquerading as curry. Just deliberate, balanced execution—or it all falls apart. As Food Network's chef and author of *Season with Authority* Marc Murphy says, "Season your food with intent." Be deliberate.

When execution works, it's magic. Talented people, aligned goals, strong communication, and clarity of purpose. When it doesn't, even a world-class idea can die on the table.

**Bottom line:** You don't get Michelin stars for trying hard—you get them for nailing the execution.

## From Netflix Chaos Monkey to Corporate Gut Checks

In engineering, "design to fail" is a compliment. It means you *expect* things to break and build systems that bounce back fast. Netflix took that to the next level with Chaos Monkey—a tool that randomly kills servers and processes in production just to make sure everything keeps running. Brutal? Yep. Smart? Absolutely.

Now, your company probably doesn't have a Simian Army. But you do have a set of tools just as effective for testing strategy, surfacing blind spots, and preparing for the inevitable market ambush: **Pre-Mortems, War Games,** and **Red Teaming.**

Let's break them down.

### Pre-Mortem Analysis: *Assume the Body's Already Cold*

This technique was a hit at the World Economic Forum in Davos when it was discussed because it was a technique anybody—

literally—could use. Instead of waiting for failure and scrambling post-mortem, you fast-forward and ask: "*It's a year from now and this project failed spectacularly. Why?*"

Pre-Mortem Analysis allows the team to imagine, think Einstein like possibilities of what could happen or could have been avoided as in market myopia. Maybe that 2.0 release is really a 1.4 when compared to the competition. Maybe the team is including some pet project feature that brings no compelling reason for a customer to buy.

**War Gaming simulates a real-world battle for market share.**

**When to use it:**

- At the start of strategic initiatives, launches, or strategy cycles.
- Before locking in budgets, roadmaps, or investor updates.
- Before committing to delivery dates and an engineering plan.

**How to do it:**

1. Assemble the cross-functional team—yes, more than engineering.
2. Assume failure is inevitable.
3. List reasons everything that could have gone wrong: missed trends, pet features, even Steve from legal.
4. Prioritize the biggest threats—the ones that matter.
5. Brainstorm fixes **now,** not after the wreckage.

**Why it matters:**

It kills false optimism, exposes inconvenient truths, and forces the team to act like grown-ups. It also separates wishful thinking from reality—and that may be the most valuable ROI of all.

## War Gaming … *Strategy with Elbows Out*

Think of it as Pre-Mortem meets roleplay—with competition, chaos, and consequences. War Gaming simulates a real-world battle for market share, letting teams test how customers, competitors, and internal factions might respond.

War Gaming is about playing to win without the real cost of doing it in the market.

I remember an exercise we did at a conference where we did a War Gaming Exercise on the topic of *What should Whole Foods do?* and recommended they get acquired by Amazon. Within the following two months, that happened.

War Games aren't party tricks. They take prep—a solid briefing book, committed people, and a couple of days to get it right. But they're worth every slide and sticky note.

**When to Use:**

- Before entering a new market or expanding into adjacent market segments.
- Before solidifying a development plan.
- During M&A planning, major pricing changes, or rebrands.
- Test how your plan affects the rest of the company's product portfolio.
- When you need to "stress test" your strategy with sharp elbows.

**How to Do It:**

1. Pick your battlefield: market, segment, scenario.
2. Get an Executive Sponsor to ensure buy-in.
3. Create a briefing book: yes, it can be 100+ slides.

4. Assign cross-functional teams to roles: your company, competitors, customers, analysts.
5. Play a few rounds—announce moves, anticipate counter-moves, debate outcomes.
6. Debrief. Document. Adjust your actual strategy.

**Pro Tip:**

Bring in a trained facilitator. Experts keep the exercise focused, fierce, and fruitful.

## Red Teaming—*Your Best Offense Is a Loyal Enemy*

Popularized by *Red Teaming* author Bryce Hoffman, Red Teaming is rooted in military intelligence. The execution of Red Teaming creates a safe space for constructive sabotage. A person designated as the **devil's advocate,** also known as "Ipcha Mistabra" (מסתברא איפכא), takes the contrary view. A Red Team's job? Tear your plan apart—on purpose—before the market does. It's a gutsy, and smart, thing to do.

**When To Use It:**

- Before major decisions, launches, or board meetings.
- When Groupthink is stifling dissent.

**How to Do It:**

1. Pick a critical initiative.
2. Assemble a Red Team—external folks work best—less Kool-Aid. Avoid the big consulting firms—they have their own agenda.
3. Give them full access, total honesty, and permission to be ruthless.

4. Let them challenge assumptions, pressure-test claims, and highlight your blind spots.
5. Don't get defensive—this is the part where you grow.

**Why It Matters:**

Innovation doesn't die from bad ideas. It dies from **smart ideas with dumb assumptions** no one dared to question.

## Designing for Failure Is Designing for the Future

None of this is about being pessimistic. It's about being prepared. The best strategies don't just survive customer contact—they survive ambushes, pivots, executive turnover, and yes, the metaphorical truck breaking down on launch day.

Whether you're scrappy or massive, startup or legacy, the tools are on the table. Use them. Because pretending failure won't happen? That's not bold—it's blind.

# key lessons

**1. Vision Without Execution Is Just Optimism Dressed as Strategy.**

The graveyard is full of great ideas that died because someone couldn't deliver.

Execution is the real MVP—and the rarest skill in the building.

**2. If You Don't Actively Stress-Test Your Strategy, Reality Will—Violently.**

Pre-mortems, red teaming, and war games aren't optional. They're unpaid insurance against corporate stupidity.

Because the market doesn't care about your feelings, your roadmap, or your optimism—only whether your plan survives first contact.

**3. The Only Way to Avoid Failure Is to Hunt It First.**

Design-to-fail, chaos engineering, pre-mortems, and war games are powerful tools.

The question is:

- Do you have the guts to use them before the actual disaster hits?
- Most teams don't—and that's why they lose.

**Pre-mortems, Red Teaming, and war games tilt the odds. But the market still throws elbows. What happens when your beautiful plan meets the beautiful mess? Welcome to the middle.**

eleven

# The Messy Middle ... Where Vision Meets Reality

When you're stuck in the messy middle, half the energy gets sucked into invisible work.

Execution. It's the line between being a hero and being a jackass. It's where the rubber hits the road, the wheat gets separated from the chaff, and promotions get made—or you get to "update your resume."

This is the moment every exec, investor, and stakeholder quietly wonders: *Can they pull it off?* It looked bulletproof in PowerPoint. The TAM was a greenfield big enough to graze a thousand unicorns. Clear Blue Ocean ahead without a hint of red. But now the Champagne's gone flat, and reality's rolled up its sleeves.

The middle is where the vision gets tested, where the team either gels or starts passive-aggressively CC'ing each other, and where execution turns into a knife fight with reality. Overinflated expectations, the wrong talent, delivery schedules based on wishful thinking —this is where they come home to roost. And it's where you find out if your "vision" is really innovation ... or just a knock-off with better marketing.

Welcome home to the messy middle. Wipe your feet on the way in, please.

## Your Mess vs. My Mess

One product team came to us for help. Their flagship was long in the tooth, and even loyal customers were starting to ask, "Great run —but what's your Act II?"

We did our homework—market trends, competitive moves, partner chatter, technology trends, comparisons and evaluations, customer feedback. Then we gave them a set of clear, data-backed recommendations on exactly where to take the next generation of product. It was bold. It was doable. It could have been a category reset and set the table for the next decade or more.

Their response? *This is a great idea, but we don't know how to do microservices.*

Our response? *This is where Amazon Web Services is going using similar technology to reach new markets.*

Their response back: *We don't know how to do this.*

And with that, the messy middle swallowed them whole.

They ditched a bold, achievable leap for the safety of building old style from scratch—slow, familiar, and doomed. While the industry started wiring together microservices to grab market share, they were stacking Duplo blocks and calling it architecture.

**Time isn't your friend. It's the undertaker.**

Nearly three years later, they finally limped out with a beta. Nobody wanted it.

It's like when you burn meat so badly on the grill, not even the dogs want it.

The market noticed. Customers started defecting to competitors who seemed to have a plan. Their once-flagship product went from the "Leader" quadrant to the "WTF" quadrant.

They tried to regroup—operative word: *tried.* Someone convinced someone else to throw good money after bad. This is the Sunk Cost Fallacy—they spent another 18 months trying to make roast beef out of horse's ass.

Market share was dropping faster than an elevator with a snapped cable. Five years late, the barely minimum viable product rolled out … and the industry had already moved on. In the messy middle, time isn't your friend. It's the undertaker.

## Tailor, Not Taylor

Another product group, another scenic detour into the messy middle.

Picture this: You buy front-row tickets to see a mega-star pop singer—the one your kid's obsessed with. You show up, lights go down … and out walks someone who *resembles* her, has the hair, the outfit—but can't carry a tune in a bucket. You'd feel a little duped, right?

Customers feel the same way about products. Expectations are set. When reality doesn't match the promise, disappointment turns to anger at warp speed.

In this case, the product group asked what they should be building next. We did the analysis, made recommendations, and they agreed—completely. This should've been an easy win.

But then the "tailoring" started. Bigger, faster, flashier. They were adding feature like they were auditioning for a new reality show: *Extreme Makeover: Product Edition.* One week it was a widget, the next a bolt-on gizmo. And every time they showed the roadmap to customers, they doubled down on the hype with delivery dates only achievable if physics took a holiday … a long holiday.

The messy middle loves this kind of optimism—it eats it for breakfast.

As the months passed, schedules slipped like greased rope. Features got chopped and thrown overboard faster than luggage on a sinking ship. By the time they finally shipped, customers weren't just underwhelmed—they felt conned. They expected the mega-pop star. What they got was a knock-off lounge act from a no-name Vegas bar.

## Rescue Missions and Triage Thinking

A friend with a venture capital firm asked me to help one of their portfolio companies get its act together. Not my usual gig, but I was between jobs and figured it might be fun.

It didn't take long to see the problem: it wasn't talent—it was focus. They were at the buffet of opportunity with a plate so overloaded it was bending in the middle. Too many "we could do this" ideas and no single "we *will* do this" decision.

Their messy middle was simple: pick one thing they could win. The venture capitalists (VC's) were worried about their investment being squandered away by indecision and lack of focus after writing the checks.

So we sat down and ran the gauntlet—market sizing, competitive analysis, partnership potentials, funding milestones, and development output. We made a rule: once the majority picked a direction, we'd all commit. No backroom pet projects. No "just in case" side hustles.

A lot of ideas landed squarely in the "could do" bucket but weren't game changers. Some were DOA—Dead On Arrival. We narrowed it to two real contenders, debated hard for a few weeks, and finally chose one. Everyone aligned. Product management built a conservative but achievable roadmap—must-haves first, nice-to-haves later. Engineering scoped a realistic plan that fit the budget.

The result? They hit every milestone. Funding secured. More capital raised. Instead of stalling in plateau city, they gained momentum—and a couple of years later, they were acquired for massive multiple by one of those potential partners we identified. People retired early.

The messy middle never had a chance. This was a team that was honest, pragmatic, and locked in. I wish more groups had that kind of maturity—reality-based execution beats daydream-based roadmaps every time.

## Data Denial and the Prisoner of Bad Assumptions

Some teams are prisoners in a jail they build themselves. The bars aren't steel. Instead, they're spreadsheets and Jira tasks. The data is right there, waving at them from across the hall, but they're too busy polishing the bars of their bad assumptions to notice.

**Data denial is lethal.**

One group I worked with had no shortage of confidence. Charts, dashboards, KPIs, orthogonal recommendations—they looked like they were running a NASA launch. Their problem? Their "data" was the marketing equivalent of a Potemkin village: carefully curated to confirm what they already believed—hint: Confirmation Bias.

We showed them customer and industry analyst feedback on their plan. Surveys. Industry trends. What the competition was pitching. Cue awkward silence, side glances, and sudden outbreaks directed at us, "We'll get back with you." Storm clouds and locusts. Not sunny meadows. They had come up with their own list of features and enhancements they wanted to build, aka "science project," not because it actually solved any customer problem. It was like watching a snow cone melting on a Texas sidewalk in July. Not pretty.

What did they do?

Instead of confronting the facts they were building something customers didn't want, they doubled down. The prisoners of bad assumptions don't want parole—they want better curtains for the cell. They tweaked messages and features to make what they created fit the narrative *they* wanted to believe. They manipulated data to support their version of the truth. This is a classic case of economist Ronald Coase's famous maxim, "if you torture the data long enough, it will confess to anything."

Meanwhile, the market was moving on without them. Nobody thought their attempt to tell people their vision was the right train to ride was cute. They wanted to go to Memphis, not data hell.

In the messy middle, data denial is lethal. If your reality check bounces, so will your customers. The only way out of the prison is to unlock the cell with facts—all of them and especially the ugly ones—and walk them out into the daylight. But that takes guts. The status quo is strong and more teams than you'd think would rather decorate the dungeon.

## The Invisible Work Problem

When you're stuck in the messy middle, half the energy gets sucked into invisible work—endless meetings, status updates, and "alignment" sessions that don't move the ball an inch. This is usually when product teams realize they're overcommitted and underperforming. Cue the scramble to jettison features off the Jira board in an attempt to "refactor" the schedule and deliverables.

If lucky, they warn their executive sponsors that the release won't be as impactful, meaning less revenue. If not, they go radio silent and hope no one notices until launch day. Their victory release becomes a partial victory.

Sometimes they rebrand a minor item as a major feature that was "reprioritized based on customer demand." The reality: it was some maintenance thing nobody actually asked for.

Now contrast that with teams that ship products on-time and as planned. You can spot them instantly: they're not obsessing over velocity charts, they're talking about customers using something real. They're solving actual problems, not imaginary ones from slideware personas. They measure success by customer adoption and their benefits achieved.

## The Optimism Trap

Running on the treadmill doesn't get you out of the gym.

It's really hard to get a team back on track with realistic expectations when they've been led to believe that being optimistic and running harder on the treadmill will bring success. They've been indoctrinated with the "we'll just work harder"—as if extra hours can fix a flawed plan.

What's needed isn't more sweat; it's a hard recalibration of the strategy and the plan. That means confronting the brutal facts, not decorating them.

And here's the kicker: most messy middles are preventable. War gaming, red teaming, and pre-mortems aren't academic exercises. They're insurance policies. They surface blind spots before you waste years chasing ghosts.

# key lessons

### 1. Vision Is Cute—Execution Is a Knife Fight.

Everyone loves the rosy PowerPoint fantasies until the messy middle shows up with deadlines, misalignment, and inconvenient realities.

This is where heroes emerge... and pretenders get exposed. Stay grounded in reality.

### 2. Fear, Denial, and Wishful Thinking Turn Bold Ideas into Slow-Motion Wrecks.

Teams choke in the middle because they cling to what's familiar, ignore the data, and treat optimism as a plan. That's when you become a garbage truck of ideas colliding with the garbage truck of reality—slow, ugly, and guaranteed to explode into a smelly disaster.

The messy middle doesn't reward hope. It punishes delusion.

### 3. Winning Teams Focus, Commit, and Confront Brutal Facts Early.

The teams that navigate the middle don't chase 20 ideas: they pick one, align hard, kill blind spots, and iterate with discipline.

That's how you go from "possible" to "acquired for massive multiples."

**Fact:** The messy middle is unforgiving. It's also where the magic happens. If you can fight through the chaos, torch the bad assumptions, and keep the crew rowing in sync, you don't just limp across the finish line. You set the pace for everyone else. You change the game.

If the middle is where most strategies die, the answer isn't more heroics—it's a better loop. The teams that win don't sprint once; they iterate relentlessly and compound.

twelve

# The Vision Loop ... Strategy That Doesn't Sit Still

To deny iteration is to deny learning.
And in business, that's a fast-track to irrelevance.

I wrote about one of my team's products in a prior chapter—the one that dethroned the legacy leaders in a 50-year-old market. It wasn't luck. It was five years of hard-fought iteration. Each release sharpened the value, expanded the capability, and pulled us closer to the endgame: market leadership.

The vision never changed. But the strategy evolved constantly—because ignoring feedback, failures, or market shifts isn't vision. It's arrogance.

## Strategy is not a plan. It's a process.

Forget the slideware. Strategy isn't a one-and-done PowerPoint deck you archive after the offsite. It's a living loop—a cycle of vision, execution, reflection, and iteration.

The vision loop is what separates the companies that *wish* for greatness from the ones that *build* toward it—one smart iteration at a time.

The reflection part means taking stock of how your product was received. Did customers love it? What was missing? How did the market and your competition react (think War Game results)? Lessons learned?

Take China's EV strategy. The vision? Global dominance. The path? Iterative execution. Each EV release is a little better. A little cheaper. A little faster. They keep building while the rest of the world keeps debating.

To deny iteration is to deny learning. And in business, that's a fast-track to irrelevance.

## Quarterly Results vs. the Long View

To call the vision loop "rinse and repeat" would be an insult. It's not routine. It's ritual. It's how empires are built—not how quarters are padded.

Too many American companies live and die by quarterly earnings. Strategies are warped to chase stock price sugar highs, not sustainable value. Vision becomes a hostage and takes a back seat to the next investor call.

Now compare that to how many Asian companies operate. They take the long view. Strategic patience. Consistent investment. Deliberate iteration. When markets dip, they don't panic—they double down. They're not playing for Q2. They're playing for the next decade or two.

And history? It tends to reward the patient.

## Amazon vs. JD.com ... Playing Different Games

Take Amazon and JD.com—two e-commerce giants, but with very different operating philosophies.

**Amazon** has long walked a tightrope between short-term investor pressure and long-term bets. To Jeff Bezos' credit, he trained Wall Street to tolerate thin margins in exchange for market dominance. But even Amazon isn't immune to quarterly pressure. They will pivot on investments quick when needed—cutting Alexa, slowing grocery store expansion, workforce reductions—all in response to investor sentiment.

On the other hand, **JD.com**—a China based entity—plays the long game. The very long game. They own their logistics network, unlike Amazon, which outsources a lot of its delivery to third parties. That's a cash-intensive, slow payback strategy. But it means tighter control, better service, and resilience. They're building infrastructure that pays dividends over decades.

**Amazon optimizes for optionality.**

**JD.com optimizes for operational excellence.**

One is nimble while the other is grounded. Different strategies. Both models work but one is more susceptible to short-term noise.

Are you preparing for the next earnings call or the next era?

### Optimizing for Optionality

When a company optimizes for optionality, it's basically saying:

**We're not locking ourselves into one bet.**
**We're buying time, flexibility, and escape routes.**

It's the corporate version of avoid hitting that "Buy Now" button in case a better price comes along.

In practical terms, this means:

- Investing in a lot of different initiatives, even if most don't pay off.
- Avoiding irreversible decisions.
- Delaying commitment until more information is available.
- Keeping cash on hand or assets liquid for when the next opportunity arrives.

Amazon is the poster child for this.

They spin up products (Fire Phone), kill them just as fast, and double down only when the data hits—like AWS (Amazon Web Services). It's toe-dipping at scale.

That's optionality.

And while optionality might make you agile, resilient to market shifts, and give the ability to pivot fast, the downsides are equally perilous. Being spread too thin, only trying things when a full-on investment is the right answer, and that some investors might tire of the "try everything" approach.

**Optionality is fine until it becomes fragmentation.**

JD.com? They're the opposite. Fewer bets. Big, deliberate plays. No backup dance—just main stage commitment.

Are you building a strategy for the freedom to pivot or focus to dominate? Both work.

You can't fake commitment and claim to be all-in.

## Portfolio Pandemonium

At one tech company, optionality became a monster. Thirteen products, four development centers across three continents, and a turf war between teams all jockeying for control. It was like herding caffeinated cats. The result? Total portfolio pandemonium.

After yanking out a few hairs, I brought in a no-BS technical lead everyone respected to help me cut through the fables versus reality. Every product had a purpose, sure, but they'd been slapped together over time like aftermarket bolt-ons. Necessary, maybe. Integrated? Not even close.

**No action.**
**No prioritization.**
**No communication.**

To customers, we were delivering a DIY car kit. They just wanted a car to drive. Meanwhile, our biggest competitor gave them one—turnkey, polished, done.

So, we killed the clutter. Consolidated and cut the portfolio from 13 down to 4. Same power under the hood, just cleaner options. Want leather or vinyl? AC or not? Tinted windows? Pick your trim, drive off the lot.

We forced the team to think and act as one—unified, streamlined, and optimized. We validated it with real customers. Their response? A relieved, "Finally."

Optionality is fine until it becomes fragmentation. What started as flexibility had become friction. We had to shift from *more options* to *better decisions*. We traded choice for clarity—and that's when we got our edge back.

## Separating Signal from the Noise: Learning What Feedback Matters

The Vision Loop runs on iteration—and iteration runs on feedback. But here's the catch: not all feedback is worth listening to. The trick is knowing which signals matter, and which ones are just noise.

Same company, different mess. My predecessor had been collecting customer feedback via enhancement requests like they were baseball cards … and then doing nothing with it. No action. No prioritization. No communication. Customer satisfaction had tanked—partly due to product, partly due to process, and a whole lot due to silence.

When I stepped in, two glaring issues surfaced fast:

- A 1,200+ backlog of enhancement requests from our user group, untouched for over five years.
- Major quality and stability issues plaguing our software.

First, we tackled the enhancement requests. I built a triage team with engineers, my technical lead. Every week, we carved out two hours to work through the list, item by item. We discussed the request, its feasibility, and gave it a disposition: yes, no, defer, already done.

It took about six months, but we got it done—and brought our findings straight to the users at the annual users group meeting. Check.

## Bugs, Bloat, and Budget Cuts

The quality problem? Trickier. We sifted through the bug reports, mapped them by severity, and traced them back to the responsible dev teams. I put a freeze on all new feature development while we got this sorted out. Fix stability first, earn trust back. Most customers understood begrudgingly. They wanted a reliable product too.

They were mad. Threatened to defect because of quality issues.

That's when we found the real issue:

**Engineering wasn't the problem. Testing was.**

Turns out, the company had slashed the QA team's budget years earlier. With fewer people and zero headcount for new testing scripts, the test suite hadn't been updated in *three years*. New features weren't even being touched—they were validated against an ancient criteria. That's not QA—that's wishful thinking. No wonder the bug escape rate went through the ceiling.

To leadership's credit, they fixed it fast. Budget restored. Headcount approved. Test coverage expanded. We re-tested the last production release ... and reduced bugs by 3,114%. Not a typo.

Customers noticed. And just like that, the needle moved.

## The Strategy Loop Never Sleeps

Strategy isn't a milestone. It's motion.

When done right, it doesn't live in a binder or get attacked by the corporate antibodies. It's baked into every decision, every customer call, every product release.

The companies that win? They never stop looping. They iterate, refine, learn, and adapt—and do it again.

Markets change. Competitors adapt. Customers surprise you. If you're not adjusting, you're delusional.

Never confuse the plan with the mission. The plan changes. The mission stays locked.

Optionality helps you survive. Iteration helps you adapt. But clarity of vision? That's what gets you across the finish line.

## Being Lugubriously Articulate

Some may think this chapter was a little lugubrious, but each situation had a happy ending. Speaking of lugubrious... before we move on to discussing Competitive Intelligence that works.

It involved **Killepitsch**—Dusseldorf, Germany's answer to Jägermeister, only 10 times stronger and twice as expensive. Greg, Jim, and I were in Düsseldorf on business, and the rule was simple: as long as you could clearly say the phrase *"lugubriously articulate,"* you could keep drinking.

Nobody knew what the hell it meant—but that was the fun. It was something only sober people could say without slobbering all over the table and themselves.

The moment you slurred it or sprayed the table, you were done.

Looking back, I still don't know what "lugubrious" actually means. Probably something orthogonal. Or pretentious. Or both.

# key lessons

### 1. Strategy Is a Loop That Never Sleeps.

Real strategy lives in motion: vision → execution → reflection → iteration.

The companies that win don't get lucky—they get better and more efficient with *every single cycle*.

### 2. Quarter-by-Quarter Thinking Is Strategy's Silent Assassin.

Asian firms double down when markets dip.

Western firms panic-cut to impress investors for 90 days: the classic "hockey stick" approach to revenue.

Only one of these builds empires that last.

### 3. The Real Advantage? Knowing Which Feedback to Use and Which to Burn.

Customers gave you the map.

QA gave you the warning signs.

Engineering gave you the truth.

Filtering signal from noise isn't insight, it's survival.

**Vision, imagination, and execution—**
**the loop only gets stronger**
**when your intel is sharper.**

**Next up:**
**how to see the field like a pro**
**and make the market play your game.**

part three

# The Opportunity: CI as a Strategic Lever

## Author's Note

# CI as a Strategic Lever

Have you ever wondered why some companies always seem a step ahead—launching products that reset the market, shaping the story customers believe, and forcing competitors into games they can't win? And why others, with the same data in front of them, get blindsided over and over?

That's the real challenge of competitive intelligence. It's not about collecting information; it's about what you *do* with it. Too many teams confuse dashboards with insight, or drown in data while the real signal slips by. Competitors flood the field with noise to throw you off balance. Patterns look obvious—until they break and leave you flat-footed. The illusion of insight can be more dangerous than ignorance.

But when intelligence becomes a lever, everything changes. Instead of reacting to the last move, you start anticipating the next. Instead of building roadmaps as checklists, you build them as battle plans—designed to trip rivals before they even take a step. Instead of mistaking activity for advantage, you sharpen your ability to separate noise from signal, and act with timing that others miss.

That's what you'll find in the chapters ahead. Stories about stepping into the enemy's shoes to see the field as they do. Lessons on filtering blind spots and anomalies that hint at shifts no one else sees. Examples of using intelligence not just to defend your position, but to reshape the game—to write the narrative, set the tempo, and make competitors burn energy in places you don't.

If Part One was about becoming strategic, and Part Two about staying strategic when the game turns hard, Part Three is about bending the game itself. It's intelligence transformed into leverage—a force that doesn't just keep you in the fight, but tilts the entire arena in your favor.

Because in the end, CI isn't homework. It's a weapon.

**For the Product Manager:**

CI isn't a report from the competitive team.

*It's how you anticipate competitor moves,*
*shape your roadmap,*
*and avoid building the wrong thing.*

**For the Strategist:**

CI isn't a quarterly deck from the competitive team.

*It's how you spot patterns,*
*frame market shifts,*
*and create asymmetry*
*that makes competitors irrelevant.*

**For the Executive/Leader:**

CI isn't just an input.

*It's an edge multiplier—*
*early warning systems, foresight muscle,*
*and the discipline of acting*
*before the obvious shows up on a dashboard.*

**CI is the practical skill**
**of outthinking your rivals in real time.**
**It's about how to use CI to win.**

thirteen

# Becoming The Enemy … The CI–Driven Product Manager

***Competitive intelligence*** and ***competitor intelligence*** are not the same thing.

I've got a bone to pick with Sun Tzu quotes—not with the man himself, but with the butchered translations floating around and used around LinkedIn and corporate slide decks.

Case in point:

**"知彼知己，百战不殆."** ***Thezhī bǐ zhī jǐ, bǎi zhàn bù dài***

*The Art of War*, new translation by Ralph D. Sawyer nails it:

**Know thy enemy and know yourself;**
**in a hundred battles, you will never be in peril.** *(Accurate)*

Unnamed Other: "If you know your personal brand and analyze your competition, success is inevitable." *So inaccurate.*

Seriously? That's not strategy—that's some influencer marketing gone rogue.

I much prefer Musashi Miyamoto. He was a strategist. Lived it. Did it. He employed a great strategy to upset Kojirō Sasaki at their duel on Ganryū Island.

## CI—Driven Product Manager

Honestly—one of the best parts of being a PM (product manager) isn't the roadmap or stakeholder meetings. It's the fight. The competitive chess match. The thrill of outsmarting the other guy.

Once the product specs are locked and dev starts doing its thing, my brain shifts gears—from building to battle master. That's when competitive intelligence becomes my weapon of choice.

But let's get something straight: **competitor intelligence** and **competitive intelligence** are *not* the same thing—even if people use them interchangeably.

### Competitor Intelligence

This is the narrow lens. It's all about them.

**Use *competitor intel* to win this quarter's deals.**

- Product
- Pricing
- Financial performance
- Leadership
- Marketing

It's reactive. Tactical. Focused on short-term play and today's threats.

### Competitive Intelligence

**Use *competitive intel* to shape next year's roadmap.**

This is the wide-angle lens. It's not just about who you are fighting—it's about the battlefield itself.

- Market trends
- Customer preferences

- Regulatory change
- Substitute products
- New entrants
- Economic and geopolitical shifts

This is how you play *tomorrow's* game. CI lets the you map blind spots, anticipate disruptions, and see moves your rivals haven't even thought of yet.

## The Product Manager's CI Formula

Use **competitor intel** to win this quarter's deals. Use **competitive intel** to shape next year's roadmap.

Smart product managers do **both.** Strategic product managers do them well. CI isn't optional—it's how you build to win.

## Becoming the Enemy

*"To know your enemy, you must become your enemy."* Whether Sun Tzu actually said that or not doesn't matter. What matters is that it's true.

**Start thinking like your rival.**

Author John Horn's *Inside the Competitor's Mindset* hits the bullseye. He uses the image of a kitten looking in the mirror who sees a lion as his reflection. The problem? Most companies do the opposite. They see a kitten and assume it's harmless. They project their own lens, biases, and assumptions onto competitors then walk into ambushes because they think they're chasing a house cat.

Musashi became Japan's greatest and most revered sword fighter based on his intense study of his opponents or enemies to the point he became them, anticipating every move and developing the right strategy for each encounter. Each strategy was custom made for its situation.

As a product manager or strategist, your job's no different. You don't just need customer empathy—you need **strategic empathy.** Think like your rival. Understand their pressure points, how they make decisions, and where they can't see clearly. That's how you predict moves before they make them.

Musashi's toolkit was strategy disguised as swordplay:

- **Deception over force:** Unnerve them before the fight starts.
- **Adaptability:** Adjust tactics to fit the threat.
- **Improvisation:** Use the terrain, the sunlight, the moment.
- **Mental advantage:** Win the mind before you draw the blade.

*The Book of Five Rings (Go Rin no Sho)* wasn't a "how to" on killing people. It was Musashi's masterclass in perception, timing, and competitive advantage.

**Channel your inner Musashi.** Stop thinking like a product manager. Start thinking like your rival—and beat them to their own move. How do you go about learning about your opponent?

## Gathering Competitive Intel Like a Pro

As a former Chairman of SCIP (Strategic and Competitive Intelligence Professionals) and Academy of Competitive Intelligence (ACI) faculty member, I've spent years showing people how to push beyond surface-level intel. In my workshops, I run a simple but powerful drill.

**Take a hypothetical manufacturing competitor and figure out their product and production capacity legally and ethically.**

Spoiler alert: You won't find it on their website or by asking your favorite GenAI. This kind of intel doesn't sit on the surface. It takes creative thinking, strategic curiosity, and good old-fashioned sleuthing.

So how do you do it?

## Techniques That Work ... Without Getting You Sued

**Job Postings:** What roles are they hiring for at that location? Engineering? Supply Chain Manager? 3PL (third-party logistics)? Chemists? Each one signals a strategic focus for their production line.

**Strategy is timing—and timing requires *anticipation.***

**Interviews & Conversations:** Talk to former and current employees, suppliers, partners, and customers. Go to that location's local job fairs and trade shows for that industry. Be curious. Competitive intelligence expert Ellen Naylor delivers a masterclass in getting people to talk in her book, *Loosen Their Lips*.

**Satellite & Public Data:** Use commercial satellite imagery (time-lapsed patterns), permit filings, EPA impact reports, construction records, and import/export data. These reveal growth, expansion, or slowdown—no drones used, that are likely illegal. Figure out the size of the building and have your plant engineers mockup a production plan on what they would do. That's real insight.

You're not looking for what they say. You're looking for what it **implies.** That's the difference between gathering data and producing real insight.

The best CI doesn't break laws—it breaks assumptions. It's about connecting the dots better and faster than your competition. And, once you've pressure-tested those insights through Red Teaming, you're not just gathering intel—you're shaping the game and ready to incorporate it into your product plans.

## Building Battle-Ready Products

Too many product managers forget about CI until *after* the roadmap is locked if they do it at all. (You know who you are.) That's like buying armor after you've already been stabbed.

Or worse—the PM only listens to the loudest salesperson, a RHiNO, who's "insight" is limited to whatever competitor they lost to last week because of one lacking feature.

Here's the problem: If you're not factoring in shifting market dynamics, evolving customer needs, and competitor blind spots, then you're swinging the bat ten seconds after the pitch hit the catcher's glove. Strategy is timing—and timing requires *anticipation.*

I've worked at companies that proudly claimed they'd "closed every competitive gap"—except for the five you could still drive a semi through. That's not strategy. That's delusion.

What is the right time for PMs to involve the CI team for insights? **Before, during, and after** the requirements cycle. Product planning without competitive insights is like the T-shirt that reads:

The Institute of Unfinished Research
has concluded that 6 out of 10 people ...

Musashi didn't wing it. He studied his opponents, the terrain, and the timing. Building battle-ready products requires the same level of rigor. You need deep thinking—and even deeper digging.

Don't build what the customer asked for.
Build what your competitor can't defend against.

## Predictive Intel: Seeing the Punch Before It Lands

Great product managers don't react—they *anticipate.* And get creative.

Product management—done right—requires a 360° view: customers, competitors, markets, government, regulations, externally; marketing, finance, supply chain, engineering and ops, internally. It's in this 360° view everything is evaluated so you don't get blindsided.

As a PM, I was in a meeting with engineering, who were musing and wondering where "Competitor Z" was heading with its next product since its current product was getting long in the tooth. What did we do?

We went to Competitor Z's job posting boards. What type of engineering talent was it looking to hire? What skill sets did it want from graduating college students? We slooked at all of the job search sites including the "careers" section on its website where it basically told us what it was building and the talent it sought. It told us about their roadmap investments since they were privately held.

Our engineering team used that intel to disrupt that competitor by hiring some of that key talent before it could—better benefits, better wages. We didn't wait for the answer—we anticipated and did our research. That's pre-emptying our cohorts—a version of bar chess with real consequences.

**If you're only reacting to what the competitors just did, you're already playing from behind.**

## Don't Just Play the Game—Design the Arena

The best PMs don't just beat the competition. They give their companies an unfair advantage. It's to change the rules of engagement so competition never has a chance in the first place.

The best PMs don't react. They build a world where competitors can't keep up.

**Designing the Arena means:**

- Launching features that force your competitors into an expensive decision.
- Pricing in a way that pressures their margins but scales with your growth.
- Creating messaging that redefines the category so *you* own the narrative.
- Building go-to-market motions that cut off their oxygen before they can respond.

It's not about being faster. It's about being smarter. Changing the terms of the fight while they're still putting on their boxing gloves.

## Musashi Didn't Just Fight—He Chose the Terrain

Musashi didn't show up early to his duel on Ganryū Island. He showed up late—on purpose. Threw Sasaki's whole mentality off. He arrived by boat, made Sasaki wait in the sun, and used a carved wooden oar as his weapon. He controlled all the variables. The **psychology,** the **timing,** the **terrain**—all rigged in his favor.

Product strategy works the same way. If you're playing by your competitor's rules—feature matching, imitation, price chasing, and playing their messaging game—you're already losing.

## Real Strategy is Asymmetrical

The most dangerous product isn't the one with the most features. It's the one that makes your competitor's roadmap obsolete. Force them into a game they're not prepared to play.

Maybe you simplify while they complicate.

Maybe you partner while they isolate.

Maybe you build fast while they're still organizing their research.

The best PMs don't just compete—they reshape the market.

**Musashi didn't just win fights.**
**He made sure no one fought him again.**

# key lessons

### 1. Those Who Ignore CI Are Just Guessing with Slideware.

If your roadmap isn't grounded in market forces, customer reality, and competitor weaknesses, you're not planning—you're hallucinating. Expect bad things if this is your approach. It won't be pretty, guaranteed.

### 2. To Outsmart the Competition, You Must First Become Them.

Musashi didn't beat opponents by force, he beat them by inhabiting their minds. He could see himself through their lens.

Great strategists and product people do the same: anticipate pressure points, blind spots, motives, and timing. That's real strategy.

### 3. CI Is About Weaponizing Information to Sabotage the Competition's Future.

Job postings? Intel.

Satellite images? Intel.

Random LinkedIn endorsements from an engineer who had too much sake? Also intel.

Real Strategists don't collect data—they build trapdoors.

Great Strategists don't compete—they rig the damn arena so the other guy falls through the floor while bragging about quarterly guidance.

fourteen

# CI is a Mindset and Weapon

The best way to beat competitors isn't always to fight them—it's to deny them air.

Forget the frameworks. Forget the templates. Forget the department. Competitive Intelligence is a mindset—and when used right, it's a weapon.

Every product starts as a spark—a vision of what could be. Then comes the ideation gauntlet: whiteboards, sticky notes, late-night debates. Eventually you land on a direction, maybe even crank out an MVP. But here's the truth—it's never one-and-done. A roadmap isn't a straight line; it's a series of traps, pivots, and reinforcements. Customers will bend it. Competitors will attack it. And if you're not building with intelligence baked in, that shiny roadmap is just a bullseye for your rivals to aim at.

A roadmap isn't just a delivery schedule. It's a war plan—designed to deny competitors room to maneuver.

## Weaponizing Weaknesses

Most companies build features to satisfy customers. Smart companies build features that customers love *and* competitors hate. That's the difference between a roadmap and a war plan.

Here's what I mean: every competitor has weak points—the features they've over-engineered, the integration they can't unwind, the sacred cow they're too stubborn to kill (status quo). Competitive intelligence exposes those cracks. Your job is to design your roadmap so you're pressing on those very bruises and making new cuts every chance you get.

At one company I worked for, a rival was obsessed with trying to maintain "feature parity." Every time we launched something new, they scrambled to copy it—months late, half-baked, and at a massive cost to them. We made that our weapon. We started deliberately launching lightweight features and made them sound huge in the market but was cheap for us to deliver. Our customers were happy. Their engineers got crushed under the weight of their own copycat treadmill. We didn't just win customers, we drained our rival's resources.

They left the market a few years later.

That's what weaponizing weakness looks like: don't just close the gaps, create ones your competitors can't close without bleeding their resources and cash.

## Pricing as Ammunition

Pricing isn't about margins. It's a weapon. Most companies treat pricing like bookkeeping: slap on a number, back it up with cost-plus math, and call it a day. But in the real world, pricing can be designed to make your competitors bleed.

**It's how you dictate the rules of engagement.**

I remember one of my products: it was premium all the way—the Lamborghini of the segment. Healthy margins. Zero interest in discounting just to chase a deal. Competitors? They were handing out 94% discounts like Halloween candy. Sales would come begging me to match, but I'd tell them the same thing: *if you want a Lambo, pay for a Lambo. If you want a Yugo, buy one—and enjoy the headaches that come with it.*

I taught them how to sell value.

Sure, we lost a few deals. But 80% of the "cheap" customers boomeranged back. Why? Because you get what you pay for—products that caught fire—literally, no updates, useless support, and one poor customer who waited three months for a replacement after a hurricane wiped out his system. Our competitor couldn't scale. They couldn't deliver. We cut off their oxygen supply by refusing to play their game. Their disgruntled customers added gas to the fire with their stories.

Sometimes people who buy cheap just need to learn the hard way. I learned it myself. Back in the '80s I shelled out $1,000 for a Quasar VCR. My friend? He bought a $125 Kmart special—every year. As the saying goes: *Kmart quality at Kmart prices.*

The point: pricing isn't just how you make money—it's how you dictate the rules of engagement. Done right, it forces your competitor into bad decisions while you keep scaling.

## Asymmetry and Market Shaping

Early in my career I was managing a reseller account that had just been acquired. Word leaked from their engineers: they were planning to build their own product instead of reselling ours. Their execs denied it at every meeting. You would have thought they were a resident in denial city.

I finally flew to their east coast HQ and sat down with the SVP. I said flat out: "*I know you're building your own product. But in the meantime, can you give me one good reason why we shouldn't both make a lot of money selling mine?*"

He looked stunned. "Are you serious?"

"Dead serious. If you build your own product, we'll cross that bridge later. But until then, let's both win."

He agreed. They eventually launched their product. It was slow, clunky, overpriced—and it flopped. By then we had strengthened our position and found other resellers to more than compensate the loss of that one reseller.

**Lesson:** Asymmetry buys you time. When you force your competitors to play your game by your rules—you buy time to outsmart them and then force them to suffer from the hand they created themselves.

## Owning the Narrative

That 50-year-old market we cracked in Chapter 9, *The Courage to See Clearly*, was also where we owned the narrative. Beyond the "make more money, save more money" benefits, we hammered a message loud and proud around flexibility, customization, space savings, and ROI—and we could prove it.

**Perception always wins.**

Our competitors were still fumbling with their old talking points while our messaging stuck like superglue to the soles of their shoes. They couldn't move. We knew we had struck a chord when the industry analysts started parroting our narrative back to their clients—positioning us as the thought leader and wondering why our rivals couldn't take the hint.

By the time Rip Van Winkle woke up and tried to imitate our story, it was too late. The analysts had already crowned the winner, and the market believed them. Game over.

**Lesson:** Once you own the narrative, your competitor is no longer fighting you—they're fighting perception. And perception always wins.

**CI isn't just about intel, it's about shaping the field so rivals can't even run.**

## Cutting Off Their Oxygen

That "best of breed" play I talked about back in Chapter 7, *Bar Chess,* was also where we cut off the oxygen for potential rivals. The ingenuity wasn't just the product approach—it was the ecosystem. We used a two-pronged approach: invite potential rivals to join the party instead of locking them out, and then make the party so good they'd be crazy to leave.

And we did it nicely. No threats, no saber-rattling. We didn't need to—we held all the cards. Our market position, our partnership with the core technology owner, and our access to a huge customer base made the choice obvious. Compete with us, and you'd struggle. Partner with us, and you'd win. The benefits of being with us outweighed the fantasy of going head-to-head.

At a later company, we did something similar by locking up key distribution players with exclusivity agreements. That forced competitors to slam the brakes on their GTM (Go To Market) plans. Instead of prime routes to market, they were stuck with tier-2 and tier-3 partners. We didn't just out sell them. We sucked the oxygen out of the room.

**Lesson:** The best way to beat competitors isn't always to fight them—it's to deny them air. When you control the ecosystem and the channels, they suffocate before the battle begins.

## Tempo and Timing

Strategy isn't about speed. It's about controlling the rhythm of the fight. Musashi mastered this. Against Kojirō Sasaki, he didn't just show up late—he showed up on his own terms, armed with a carved oar for length parity instead of a shorter sword for the battle. The result? Sasaki's rhythm broke before the fight even begun.

**Each move shifts the rhythm in your favor.**

Companies have rhythms too. Big ones are the easier: spring and fall launches, annual conferences, predictable earnings calls. They plan their moves like clockwork, which means you can plan to throw them off balance.

How?

- **Disrupt their cycles:** preempt their big announcement with one of your own.
- **Launch when they can't respond:** layoffs, turmoil, executive turnover/vacancies, or distractions. Turn their bad news into your good news.
- **Beat them to the punch:** announce first, force them into reactive mode.
- **Expose bad timing:** show their launch is too early for the market or already obsolete.

Each move shifts the rhythm in your favor and forces them onto their back foot.

**Lesson:** Strategy is rhythm. If you control the tempo, you control the fight. Too early wastes effort. Too late cedes ground. But strike in the pocket—when they can't respond and customers are ready—and even a small move can feel like a knockout punch to them.

### Psychological Warfare

Sometimes the best way to win isn't with features or pricing—it's by messing with your rival's head. Competitors are just companies full of people, and people crack. They overreact, they chase shadows, they double down on bad bets just to save face. That's where competitive intelligence becomes psychological warfare.

I've seen it firsthand. One time we hinted at a "major feature release" coming in the next quarter. Truth? It was a minor upgrade. But our competitor scrambled like it was the Second Coming. They pulled engineers off core projects to figure out what we were doing and develop a counter measure that delayed their own roadmap, confusing sales and their customers. All because we got into their head. By the time they figured it out, they were months behind—and we had stolen and controlled the narrative.

Psychological warfare doesn't mean lying or making things up. It's about leveraging perception as a weapon. Drop hints, just enough half-truths, control the analyst chatter, and you'll watch your competitor tie themselves in knots.

**Lesson:** Sometimes the easiest way to win is to let your competitor punch themselves in the face.

## The Roadmap as a War Plan

Last topic before we move on. Most companies treat their roadmap like a project plan: dates, features, and a neat Gantt chart to make everyone feel warm and fuzzy. But a roadmap isn't a to-do list. It's a war plan.

Every feature, every release, every sequence is a strategic decision. You're not just shipping a product—you're choosing where to strike, when to defend, and how to deny your competitors room to maneuver.

Weaponize their weaknesses. Set pricing traps. Own the story. Lock up oxygen. Control the rhythm. Get into their head. That's not a roadmap—that's a war plan.

That's what a war plan does—it turns random lists of features into deliberate strikes.

**Lesson:** A roadmap without competitive intelligence is just a schedule. A roadmap built with CI is a weapon. And the best strategies don't just keep you in the game—they make sure your competitors never want to play again. Just like Musashi.

## Roadmaps don't win markets. War plans do.

A roadmap built as a war plan only works if your team can see the battlefield. Too many organizations hand teams a strategy like it's IKEA furniture—here's the parts, here's the instructions, now go assemble it. But real strategy isn't handed down, it's built into how people think.

CI isn't homework, it's ammo. Use it right and your products don't just launch—they land like bombs.

# key lessons

### 1. A Roadmap Is Map Designed to Make Competitors Bleed.

Most teams build for customers.

Smart teams build for customers **and** to inflict maximum pain on rivals.

Every feature should be a strike, not a checkbox.

### 2. Weaponize Their Weak Points—Don't Just Close Gaps, Create New Ones.

Spot the overbuilt module, the sacred cow, the copycat addiction—then exploit it.

Make them chase. Make them spend. Make them *suffer.*

They don't lose when you win ... they lose when they burn resources trying to keep up.

### 3. Strategy Is Rhythm—Control the Tempo and You Control the Fight.

Strike before they're ready.

Launch when they can't react.

Accelerate when they're distracted.

Let them punch themselves in the face.

Musashi didn't just fight—he choreographed the battle. So should you.

**If your team can't see competitor moves, market shifts, and the subtle cues that signal change, then all you've got is a laminated plan taped to the wall. The real edge comes when your team learns to see for themselves—spot patterns, anticipate moves, and think like strategists instead of task executioners.**

**That's where we go next.**

fifteen

# Teach Your Team to See

Our ability to see the future is shaped—and limited—
by our own experience and biases.

Strategic intelligence isn't about collecting facts. It's about catching patterns before your competitors, before your markets, and sometimes before your leadership even knows they're forming.

That's the real edge.

Ever noticed how some people justseem to know what's about to happen?

They're not psychic. They're strategic. That's informed anticipation.

They listen differently. They connect the dots others ignore. They spot the early signals buried in customer complaints, subtle shifts in competitor behavior, sales dynamics, or an exec's tone in a tense meeting.

And they act while everyone else is still staring at the whiteboard.

That's *not* luck.

- A CI-driven person preempts competitor moves and shapes the roadmap.

- The strategic professionals turn the lens inward to analyze their own career trajectory.
- Great mentors don't just teach—they share patterns.
- Negotiators who win? They've read the room five moves ahead.

What ties it all together?

**Pattern recognition**

The meta-skill that transforms noise into insight. That makes decisions feel obvious in hindsight.

## Strategy Is a Gestalt Skill

Gestalt is the idea that the whole is greater than the sum of its parts. That's what strategic intelligence is, at its core.

Anyone can list facts. But seeing the relationship, dynamics, timing, and intent behind those facts? That's the leap from information to insight—from dashboard to direction.

When interviewing candidates, I test for this. Not with a résumé quiz—but with pattern-recognition puzzles. Roger, my first mentor, tested me the same way before offering me a job as a college intern. He wanted to know if I could figure out things without needing handholding.

People with strong gestalt instincts don't need micromanagement. They think in systems, not silos.

The good news? Gestalt thinking can be developed. I've brought in groups like TFSX, formerly Kedge, to help my teams build their "natural foresight" muscle. The results? Sharper thinking. Better filters. More strategic action.

One session stuck with me: the team was asked to evaluate a future scenario. The Millennials said, "Yeah, this could totally happen." The Boomers: "No way. Not realistic." Same data. Different filters. Different points-of-view based on experience.

The insight? Our ability to see the future is shaped—and limited—by our own experience and biases.

Which means if you want to recognize patterns others miss, you need to start by challenging your own capabilities. I've taken LBL Strategies' "Mastering Foresight" class taught by expert and author, Robin Champ, to help sharpen my skills.

**Strategic insights aren't about isolated facts. It's about strategic perception.**

## Dashboard Dependencies

**No one asked the critical question: *Why?***

It's not about the data. It's about the interpretation, or misinterpretation.

One of my teams built end-of-quarter dashboards showing how we stacked up again the competition. Compete volume. Win/loss by product line. Six quarters look back. Classic CI housekeeping.

And every quarter, top-line revenue kept growing. Cue the party hats.

But something didn't sit right.

We dug deeper and saw that while revenue was rising, the number of opportunities was shrinking slowly, quarter by quarter. Fewer deals. Just bigger ones leading to false trends.

The problem? Everyone focused on the green bars going up. No one asked the critical question: *Why?*

That's the risk of dashboard dependence. If you're not looking critically—and at the whole picture—you'll celebrate the wrong signal and miss the one that matters.

Dashboards don't think.
That's your job.

## Seeing Around Corners

Seeing around corners isn't magic. It's having an early warning system—the strategic version of a tornado siren. Something that says: *"Hey, you might want to take a look at this before it hits."*

Because by the time a trend shows up on a dashboard, it's too late. The game has moved on.

My team spent lots of time building early warning systems.

**Early warning systems matter.**

What we found? Competitors and markets leak signals—sometimes 18-24 month ahead of their big moves. If you know how to collect and interpret the clues, they're practically broadcasting their next play.

We presented our approach at a 2019 conference. Afterward, a guy from "the defense sector" pulled us aside. He gave us a nod. "You're on the right track. This is exactly how the big players do it."

That's a good kind of goosebump moment. Validation from someone who doesn't usually validate much and doesn't identify where they're from.

We used this system to make predictions in 2020 about what 2025 would look like. Companies. Competitors. Technologies.

**AI?** Check.

**Quantum computing?** Check?

**Leading companies?** Check.

**Accuracy?** 96 percent.

Early warning systems matter. Because no competitor is going to hand you their strategic roadmap. But they will leave breadcrumbs—hiring patterns, patent filing, org changes, messaging shifts. You just need to know how to see them.

Let's be clear: these systems don't run themselves. They're not magic eight balls. You have to train the model, apply heuristics, correct for bias, and separate signal from noise. It's very noisy out there. It's work. But when it's done right? It's the closest thing to time travel you'll ever get.

## What Is the Illusion of Insight?

It's when we mistake data *presentation* for data *understanding* and its insights.

You've been there: the chart goes up in a meeting and everyone nods solemnly. Numbers look clean, trends appear obvious, and someone declares: *"Looks like we are winning in the East region."*

Maybe that bump is just one whale customer with a huge deal. You know, the kind everyone gets excited about and celebrates. Or maybe it's a timing quirk. Or maybe last quarter's comp was so bad that *anything* looks like growth.

This is the illusion of insight: believing you've understood the "why" behind the data … when you're really just staring at the "what."

**Why It's Dangerous:** Because it kills curiosity. It stops questions from being asked. People think they've already got the answer, so they stop looking deeper. That's how blind spots form. That's how companies get blindsided by competitors, market shifts, or internal breakdowns.

## Why Anomalies Are Gold

Most people ignore outliers. I chase them.

Anomalies get dismissed as noise. A glitch in the matrix, a one-off, "probably data error." But that's exactly why they matter. They break the pattern and status quo. And when that happens, it usually means the game is about to change.

One of my team members flagged something odd once—a no-name startup supposedly in stealth mode. Market whispers, scattered hints. But what we pieced together was clear: they weren't just solving a problem differently. They were rewriting the rulebook.

We ran the analysis. Fragmented inputs. Duct-taped assumptions. But the conclusion? Solid. We briefed the product team.

They laughed.

The Chief Technology Officer backed us. He got it. But he was ignored too.

Eighteen months later, product team finally woke up. They scrambled to build a copycat. But by then, the startup had a 30-month head start and never looked back.

The result? We went from market leader to follower. Then to slow follower. Then to forgotten.

All because an anomaly looked inconvenient.

**Lesson:**
**Ignore the outliers, and you won't miss the future.**
**You'll get stream rolled by it.**

## When the Pattern Breaks

Sometimes the most important signal isn't the pattern—it's when the pattern suddenly stops.

A competitor stops filing patents. A partner goes radio silent. A product line that's been consistent for years starts flailing like it's being run by a drunk octopus.

Those aren't quirks. They're tremors. And they usually signal something deeper: internal chaos, resource drain, loss of leadership, unprofitability, or all the above.

**That's not slippage. That's distress.**

We saw this in one of our most contested segments. Competitor product launches missed ... then slipped again ... and again. Release dates got shuffled like a blackjack dealer on speed. Roadmaps shrank. Feature sets got trimmed down like someone has hit "undo" three times too many. We saw the pattern occurring over and over. Different companies, same problem.

That's not slippage. That's distress.

We pounced. We reminded customers where *our* investments were going. Stability. Security. Long-term value. We didn't just sell our product—we sold our momentum. And we positioned their instability as our opportunity.

It worked. Customers didn't just start asking questions—they started asking us for quotes.

## Teach Your Team to See

One person spotting patterns is helpful.

A whole team spotting them? That's a force multiplier.

But here's the problem: most teams are trained to execute, not interpret. They chase Key Performance Indicators (KPIs) like a dog chases their favorite bone. Stay in their lanes. Hit the numbers. That's fine for operations. But useless for strategy.

Pattern recognition demands something else: curiosity, context-switching, cross-functional thinking. The willingness to challenge assumptions and ask, "What does this mean?"

That's why I trained my team to look beyond the job description. I'd assign competitor press releases, earnings reports, product announcements, patent filings—not to summarize, but to interpret. The task wasn't, "What did they say?" It was, "What are they planning next—and what should we do about it?"

We even ran internal war games. Teams were split up and told to think like our competitors—strategy, positioning, responses. That simple shift changed how they saw the game. They started anticipating, not just reacting.

They just didn't understand the value of strategic thinking. They internalized it. That's the difference between reading a map and knowing how to navigate.

**You can't build foresight with people who only know how to look backward.**

# key lessons

**1. If You Can't See Patterns—You're Just Guessing With Confidence.**

Most people don't lack intelligence—they lack *perception.*

They stare at dashboards like they're horoscopes and call it insight.

Meanwhile, the real strategists are picking up signals from tone shifts, market tremors, random anomalies, and competitor breadcrumbs scattered 24 months before the "official announcement."

Seeing isn't magic—it's refusing to be strategically blind on purpose.

**2. Anomalies Aren't Glitches—Ignoring Them Is Self-Harm.**

Anomalies are the strategic gods tapping you on the shoulder saying,

**"Hey, idiot—something's coming."**

Ignore anomalies and you don't just miss the future: you get steamrolled by it.

**3. Most People Have Blindfolds Held On with Industrial Zip-Ties.**

Let's stop pretending the inability to see patterns is a small flaw. It's strategic malpractice.

Some folks stare at dashboards like they're reading ancient ruins and proudly announce insights like: "Revenue is up!"

No, genius—a whale deal sneezed, and you mistook it for market movement. Real strategists see the tremors before the earthquake—because they're actually looking.

sixteen

# The Illusion of Insight ... and How to Kill It

Real insights scream:
"Pay attention—act now!"

Remember those old Magic Eye books? The trippy ones full of random dots and swirls where—if you stared long enough—you'd suddenly see a hidden dolphin or spaceship pop out? The catch was, once you spotted it, you couldn't unsee it. Your brain locked on. Game over.

That's the trap of the so-called "insight." Once we latch onto a pattern, we stop looking for what else might be hiding in plain sight. We confuse the first thing we see as being the only thing there is.

That's the illusion of insight. And in strategy, it's deadly.

## Run the "So What?" Test

An insight that doesn't change your behavior isn't an insight—it's trivia.

Dashboards, Key Performance Indicators (KPIs), and other metrics are dangerous because they *feel* like insight. They're safe.

They're factual. They look real. But that's the trap—they don't create urgency. They don't make you pull back the curtain to see if the Wizard is real … or just some guy yanking levers.

I've watched executives cheer because their Net Promoter Score (NPS) ticked up two points. Big deal. *So what?* Did churn drop? Did marketshare increase? Or is it just noise dressed up as progress.

Feeling good doesn't move the business. Results do.

The problem with dashboards is they often substitute for action. They're pretty—lines, bars, colors. Eye candy. But unless you dig into what they *mean*, they're useless. Real insights scream: "Pay attention—act now!" They sharpen war plans, not decorate walls.

Is revenue climbing while the market is shrinking? If you're only staring at the green line, you'll be blindsided when the tide goes out. The data was there—you just didn't see it.

If churn jumps 20%, the *so what* is simple: fix pricing, double down on retention, redo onboarding. That's not trivia. That's insight.

## Check for the Second Dolphin

Midway through my career, a smaller competitor tried a stunt that rattled our segment. "Smaller" is relative—we weren't big either, just slightly bigger than them. Meanwhile, the two tech giants owned 80% of the market. Think Papa Bear, Mama Bear … and a bunch of scrappy cubs.

**That dolphin might actually be a shark.**

Competitor Z wanted to get attention and be seen as a real player, so they published an industry benchmark with an outrageous claim—like claiming they could run a mile in two minutes flat. Everyone scoffed but secretly wondered: *could it be true?* That was the **first dolphin**—the thing everyone sees and either applauds or dismisses it.

We didn't stop there. We tore apart their claim and found the trick: creative math. They hadn't run the full mile—they sprinted a quarter mile in 30 seconds and extrapolated. By that logic, they could've claimed three miles in six minutes. Ridiculous. That was the **second dolphin**—the hidden truth you only find if you look deeper.

Here's the twist: our engineers took that gauntlet seriously. They *did* figure out how to hit the equivalent of a mile in two minutes in real customer environments, with real data. Suddenly the industry was in a three-year benchmark war, and we owned the narrative. Our numbers were real, repeatable, and public.

Lesson? The first dolphin is the flash claim. The second dolphin is the deeper reality that opens up opportunities—if you're willing to look. Tech is full of these "lab-only" performance claims that never survive under careful scrutiny or real customer environments in the light of day. Caveat emptor: don't take the first number, headline, or data point as gospel. Look again. Because if you don't, that dolphin might actually be a shark.

**Illusions are more dangerous than no insight at all.**

## Interrogating Assumptions

I've always found it fascinating how often people toss out absolute statements that nobody bothers to challenge. They're declarative. They sound authoritative, fact-based, but most of the time they're smokescreens for hidden agendas or lazy thinking.

Take the classic: *"People fear failure."* Really? Maybe what they fear isn't the failure itself, but the cost of the failure—reputational damage, lost bonuses, or wasted effort. Or the equally hollow: *"Customers always want more features."* Maybe, but if your product can't stay online, they'd trade ten new bells and whistles for a system that works.

The danger is that when you accept these declarative statements at face value, you stop asking questions. You let someone else's assumptions become your strategy. And that's how bad bets get made.

### Correlation ≠ Causation

Assumptions can make people lazy. They tempt you to mistake **correlation for causation.**

During the pandemic, cable pundits loved the take: *Company B sold more than Company A, therefore B's product is superior.*

Wrong. Do not pass GO, do not collect $200.

**One coincident is not a cause.**

Maybe Company A had supply-chain issues. Maybe Company B ran a fire-sale promotion to clear old inventory about to go stale. Maybe demand shifted to a channel Company A didn't serve. Same chart, different story than reported.

Seasonality does the same thing. "Sales are up—our new feature is selling like hotcakes!" It's December. Maybe. Maybe not.

Worse, there's **reverse causation**—smart (or manipulative) people make event A look like it caused B when the reverse is the actual truth. (See manufactured pretexts throughout history.) Don't let neat narratives replace evidence.

#### Quick kills for the correlation illusion

- What else moved? (promo, channel mix, competitor outage, global trade issues)
- Check base and seasonality

- Look for a reason: how could X cause Y to happen?
- Lag time: does X lead Y over time, or do they just tradeoff with each other?
- Look for a contradiction where X changed and Y didn't—what happened?

**One coincident is not a cause.
If you can't explain the how, you don't have the why.**

## Once Is a Data Point, Twice Is a Coincidence, Three Is a Trend

### ... aka beware of the Echo Chamber

This is a long-standing joke in the analyst community. Sadly, it happens more often than not.

**Challenge sacred cows.**

Analysts and vendors need each other. That dependency breeds **echoes.** A startup whispers "unicorn," analysts repeat it, the company quotes the analysts, and the loop amplifies until the whisper sounds like truth. Jordan Peterson mentions this in the opening chapter of his *12 Rules for Life,* and how the same amplification can affect people's lives.

Analysts are also human and can start chasing shiny objects to have bragging rights being the first proclaiming the startup is a unicorn. Often, this happens prematurely.

The problem is sometimes the unicorn turns out to be a minotaur. The magic eye lead effect leads the viewer to imagine a single horn and voilà—the illusion of the unicorn is born.

When the unicorn runs out of money, folds, or delivers a half-baked product, despite the hype, the analyst community does its mea culpa and moves on to the next shiny object.

This is why many people—me included—take what analysts say with a grain of salt. They are, in fact, one data point. If you rely on one data point for determining your strategy, you're asking for trouble.

Tips to ensure you have a clear view of the horizon:

- Do your own homework; don't rely on analysts alone.
- References—talk with their customers and rivals for a perspective.
- Use knowledge platforms that aggregate data, news gathering software.
- What is true or not true 90 days later?

**Repetition is not validation.**

If your sources aren't independent, you don't have a trend. You have a mirror.

## Bringing Insights Together

Having insights isn't the end game. Making sure they survive interrogation is. Here's how you keep yourself from falling for the illusion of insight:

### 1. Flip the Claim

If someone says, "Customers want more features," flip it on its side: "Customers want fewer features." Now you're forced to think—when is less actually more? Hint: when simplicity beats complexity. Flipping the statement forces you to challenge sacred cows.

### 2. The Counterfactual Drill

If your insights are true, there should be things you don't see. If churn is really due to price, then happy customers shouldn't be leaving despite premium pricing. If they are, something else is going on. Hunting for the missing evidence keeps you honest.

3. **The Second-Source Standard**

   No single data point should drive strategy. Back up quantitative data with qualitative data. Balance customer interviews with partner feedback. If an analyst says, "the market is shifting," check what customers they are talking about and who's buying. If you can't triangulate it, it's not an insight.

4. **Pressure-Test It**

   Before you act, throw it against a wall. Red Team it: list the top three ways this insight could be dead wrong. If it crumbles easily, congratulations. You probably saved millions and avoided a very awkward future discussion. If it holds up, then it's worth betting on.

Flip the claim. Run the counterfactual. Demand a second source. Pressure-test it until it breaks or prove it belongs in your plans.

Because here's the truth: illusions of insight are more dangerous than no insight at all. At least when you have nothing, you know it. Illusions make you confident in the wrong direction. They make you double down on bad bets, waste quarters of execution, and celebrate illusions.

The companies that win aren't the ones with the prettiest dashboards or the loudest analysts. They're the ones who keep asking: *So what? What else? What am I missing that I don't see?* They're the ones that don't stop at the first dolphin—they keep looking until they know it's really a dolphin, a shark, or just a shadow in the water. Instead of a unicorn, maybe it's a minotaur wearing a party hat.

**Lesson:** Kill the illusion early. If an "insight" doesn't change behavior, it's just noise. Insights exist to sharpen war plans, not decorate walls.

Strategy isn't about spotting the first dolphin in the dots. It's about checking whether it's really a dolphin—or just a shark in disguise. Kill the illusion, then act. Because the battlefield is full of noise, and the only edge is knowing what signals matter and when to move.

# key lessons

## 1. If You Don't Look for the Second Dolphin, the First One Will Eat You Alive.

Competitor claim looks strong? Cute.

Flip it, tear it apart, recreate it, reverse engineer it, interrogate it until it cries.

Sometimes the big "performance claim" is just **creative math wearing cologne to smell good.** And sometimes, when you actually look deeper, you discover:

- the trick
- the opportunity
- the angle
- the blind spot ... or the fact that your competitor is faking half their story.

If you don't question the first dolphin in reality, you might be staring at a shark with a mask on.

## 2. Unchallenged Assumptions Turn Smart Teams into Echo Chambers of Idiocy.

"People fear failure."

"Customers always want more features."

"Sales are up, so our strategy is working."

These aren't insights—they're bumper stickers for lazy thinkers. Every unchallenged assumption becomes a landmine.

If your team treats declarative statements as gospel, you're not doing strategy—you're just LARPing it.

## 3. Illusions Direct You into Oncoming Traffic.

False insight is more dangerous than no insight. When you know nothing, at least you know you know nothing.

When you believe the illusion, you double down confidently in the wrong direction while the market prepares for you to fail. Spectacularly.

Kill the illusion early—or it will kill your execution later.

seventeen

# Signals, Noise, and Timing

The trick is knowing the difference
between a spark and a fire.

Pilots live and die by their radar. Radar doesn't just show the enemy—it shows weather, terrain clutter, and the occasional phantom blip. If you can't tell the difference, you'll fire at clouds or fly straight into a mountain. Strategy works the same way. Everyone can see the blip. The advantage goes to the ones who know which ones are noise, which ones are real, and when to act on them.

The signals are almost always there. Sony saw tapes and CDs fading but clung to the Walkman, leaving room for Apple's iPod + iTunes. Sears invented the catalog but ignored online retail until Amazon buried them. Detroit heard the call for fuel efficiency and let Japan run away with the fuel-efficient smaller car market. Print media watched readership migrate online and still doubled down on paper. Taxis saw ride-share apps and bet on regulation instead of innovation.

Some barely survived. Others disappeared into the abyss. All of them had the signals on their radar. But comfort, arrogance, and legacy profit streams made it easier to ignore the storm.

That's what ignoring signals looks like—sipping iced tea in the yard while the tornado siren screams *take cover.*

## Filtering the Static to Gain Strategic Advantage

The world is noisy. AI deepfakes, manipulated headlines, endless dashboards. Everyone's shouting, and half of it are lies. The danger isn't that you don't hear—it's that you hear too much. The loudest signals aren't always right, and the faint ones aren't always wrong.

That's where asymmetric data comes in. Companies with richer, timelier signals hold the high ground. GenAI is only accelerating this—creating AI "factories" that boost up weak signals, filter the noise, and spit out advantage. Think real-time pricing, early-warning sensors, customer lock-in, or negotiation leverage—all tilted to your advantage because you know something your rival doesn't.

Amazon's "only 5 left" trick isn't magic. It's signal exploitation. Meta knows where you pause on a scroll—and feeds you more of it. That's asymmetric data weaponized.

### Countering Asymmetric Data

What if you're the smaller player? You still have moves.

- **Alliances:** pool intel with partners to triangulate truth.
- **Reverse Engineering:** dissect competitor claims—the second dolphin style.
- **War Gaming:** stress-test your moves against rival responses.
- **Transparency:** flip the script: show customers your data to build trust.

### Example: Linux vs. Microsoft

In the late '90s and early 2000s, Microsoft had asymmetric data power. They owned the desktop, knew the customer base, and could freeze the market with pre-announcements. Smaller rivals had no chance playing by those rules.

But the open-source community flipped the script. Linux wasn't just software—it was transparency as a weapon supported by an ecosystem of its own. The code was open for anyone to see, audit, improve, and share. Suddenly, Microsoft's black-box advantage looked like a liability. Enterprises started saying: *"Why pay a giant to lock us in when we can see exactly how Linux works—and improve it ourselves?"*

By pooling their resources with alliances across IBM, Red Hat, universities, and volunteers, the "weaker side" created triangulated data advantage. Microsoft couldn't stop them with vaporware—because the product was already out there, free, and improving daily.

**Lesson:** Sometimes the counter to asymmetric data isn't bigger data—it's transparency. If you can make your rivals' secrecy look like weakness, you've tilted the battlefield.

## False Positives, False Negatives

False signals are like fighter pilots chasing phantom blips while missing stealth bombers.

**A false positive signal burns resources where you end up chasing mirages.**

Picture this: you're walking a Parisian street, craving boeuf bourguignon. You whisper to your glasses, *"Find me a café nearby."* Instantly a heads-up display floats in front of your eyes—a five-star map, glowing reviews, prices, and your glasses asking, *"Do you want me to make a reservation?"*

That was the dream of Augmented Reality (AR) in 2012. And Google Glass was born. RIP 2015.

What happened? Glass looked like the future, but it was a false positive. The signal was there—convenience, AR, voice commands

—but it ignored the context. People weren't ready to walk around with cameras strapped to their faces. Privacy concerns, clunky hardware, and a lack of a killer app ecosystem killed it quickly.

Now flip it. A classic false negative: Apple's touchscreen keyboard in 2007. Blackberry scoffed at the idea and laughed it off. "No business user will type on glass." They dismissed the weak signal that customers valued screen space more than plastic keys. That miss cost them the market.

That's the danger. A false positive burns resources chasing mirages. A false negative blinds you to the wave that's about to crush you. The job of strategy isn't to avoid all mistakes—it's to know the difference between noise dressed as a signal, and a weak signal that's about to roar.

### The Window of Opportunity

Not all signals stay fresh. Some decay into fads; others amplify into megatrends. The trick is knowing the difference between a spark and a fire.

Remember 3D TV? Around 2010, Samsung, Sony, LG, and Panasonic bet the farm. CES was full of flashy demos. Broadcasters promised 3D sports. Blu-ray players shipped with 3D logos. It looked like the future. Then it flamed out. Why? High costs, clunky glasses, eye strain, limited content, and a miserable user experience. Novel? Yes. Practical? No. Sparks don't last.

Now look at Netflix. They spotted the deeper signal: convenience beats format. Streaming didn't need new glasses; it needed better bandwidth. By the time households had faster internet, Netflix was ready with on-demand content at a price that undercut cable and nuked Blockbuster's late fees. What started as a "nice to have" quickly became the default. That's not a spark—that's a fire.

## MiniDisc vs. iPod ... Sparks vs. Fires

In the late '90s, Sony hyped the MiniDisc as the next evolution of music. Smaller than CDs, rewritable, and "future-proof." The problem? Nobody cared. Discs were expensive, recorders clunky, and the format sat awkwardly between CDs and nascent market of MP3s. It solved no real problem. A spark, not a fire.

**Fads create noise; trends solve problems.**

Then came Apple's iPod in 2001. Same category: portable music. But Apple heard a different signal. People didn't want smaller discs; they wanted *all their music in their pocket*. Add iTunes for easy loading, the click wheel for navigation, and a market line that nailed customer needs—*"1,000 songs in your pocket."* That wasn't a gimmick, it was fuel poured on a fire.

Sony had the tech advantage, but Apple had the signal clarity. One faded into trivia. The other reshaped the industry.

**Lesson:** Fads create noise; trends solve problems. The winners aren't the ones who chase sparks, they're the ones who stockpile fuel and wait for the fire to catch.

## When Rivals Generate Noise

Competitors don't just fight with products—they fight with perception. And sometimes, that means flooding the market with noise.

Think about walking into a car dealership. You mention you're looking at another brand because it has Feature X. Without missing a beat, the salesperson fires back: *"Oh, we're launching that next year."* Translation: maybe they are, maybe they aren't—but their goal is to stall you, cloud your judgment, and keep you from defecting today.

The same tactic plays out at scale in business: pre-announcements, vaporware, and "roadmap theatre." Competitors seed promises they can't deliver, or can't deliver *yet*, to freeze customers, distract analysts, or burn your development cycles chasing shadows. It's not about truth—it's about misdirection.

I saw this happen repeatedly in high tech. Here's the catch: it only works once. Deliver late, or never, and your credibility is toast. Customers don't forgive vapor. They remember. And when it's time to vote with their wallets, they'll vote you out.

### Classic Vaporware Moves

This isn't new. Microsoft practically perfected the "announce-to-freeze" tactic in the 1990s. If a competitor was about to launch something disruptive, Microsoft would rush out an announcement: "*We've got a better version coming soon.*" Sometimes they had code in a lab. Sometimes it was just a PowerPoint slide deck making you think it was coming. But it was enough to make customers hesitate. That pause was all they needed to keep rivals from gaining traction.

Oracle used to do it too. Whole product lines and roadmaps were "announced" years before a working version was ever shipped. By the time reality caught up, competitors often lost momentum.

Tesla also leaned on "announcement theatrics." Think Cybertruck. Roadster refresh.

### How to Counter Competitor Noise

1. **Call Their Bluff:** When a rival announces something vaporous, go straight to customers and reframe it: "*That's nice, but how does it help you today?* We have it working now."

2. **Proof Over Promises:** Bring demos, case studies, references. Real beat rumored every time. Customers can smell the difference.

3. **Flip the Narrative:** Turn their pre-announcement into a weakness: *"If they're promising it for next year, it means they don't have it now."* Is the customer willing to bet their business on a promise without a kiss?
4. **Build Credibility:** If you promise, deliver. Consistency and a track record kill competitor noise faster than anything else.

**Lesson:** Noise is cheap. Delivery is priceless. Competitors can stall the market with vapor once, but if you show up with proof, they've just handed you an opening to own the narrative.

## Signals Require Interpretation

Five Man Electrical Band had a hit single song about signs, how to read them, and what they mean.

They could've just as easily been talking about business signals.

The world is full of signs: customer surveys, analyst reports, competitor press releases, quarterly trends, social chatter. Some are flashing neon warnings. Some are dead ends. Some are noise dressed up as wisdom. The problem? Signals don't speak for themselves. They require interpretation.

A rising Net Promoter Score (NPS)—is it proof of loyalty, or just people happy with the latest discount? A surge in competitor hiring—are they expanding into a new market, or just replacing turnover? A dip in your sales pipeline—is it a market slowdown, or just a sloppy quarter from the field?

The signal itself is neutral. The meaning comes from how you read it. And this is where companies get into trouble: they treat raw signals as truth instead of interrogating what they actually mean.

Blockbuster didn't miss the Netflix signal. They saw it loud and clear. By 2000, Netflix was knocking on their door, practically begging to be acquired. Blockbuster's executives interpreted the rise of DVDs-by-mail and streaming as a fringe play instead of a major market shift: inconvenient, niche, and not scalable compared to their brick-and-mortar empire.

Their mistake wasn't blindness. It was bad interpretation. They thought the signal meant "a quirky alternative" when in fact it meant "the death knell of late fees and in-store video rental." By the time they realized Netflix was reshaping customer expectations around convenience and cost, the siren had become a tornado.

We're not in Kansas anymore.

## Bringing It Together: The Rhythm of Strategy

Signals aren't the hard part. Everyone sees the blips. The edge comes from filtering the noise, interpreting correctly, and moving at the right moment. That's the rhythm of strategy. Move too early, you waste fuel. Move too late, you're a casualty. Move in the pocket—with clarity, confidence, and timing—and the market thinks it was inevitable.

That rhythm is what separates sparks from fires, fads from megatrends, survivors from the ash heap. Next, we'll look at the behaviors that make strategies endure long after the first shot is fired.

We're talking about reshaping the market.

# key lessons

### 1. Asymmetric Data Is a Weapon and If You Don't Have It, Congratulations: You're the Target.

Amazon's "Only 5 left!"

Meta tracking where you hesitate on a thumb scroll. Real-time pricing manipulation. Early-warning micro-signals.

This isn't analytics—it's **psychological warfare with better UX.**

If you're a smaller player, you need alliances, transparency, and reverse-engineering just to survive.

Because in asymmetric warfare, the side with the data doesn't fight fairly. In fact, they don't fight at all: They *win before the battle even starts.*

### 2. Noise Isn't Dangerous—Believing Noise *Is* a Signal Will Ruin Your Career.

Fake scarcity alerts. AI-generated nonsense.

Dashboards vomiting green bars like a St. Patrick's Day parade.

Some signals whisper truth. Most signals scream lies.

If you can't tell the difference, you're not "data-driven" —you're a highly educated weather vane.

Competitors will run circles around you while you chase phantom blips like a rookie pilot firing missiles at clouds.

### 3. False Positives Will Bankrupt You; False Negatives Will Bury You.

Google Glass? False positive: the future arrived wearing a cyborg headset nobody wanted.

Blackberry laughing at the iPhone's keyboard? False negative: and the last laugh they ever had.

Chasing the wrong signal wastes years. Dismissing the right signal destroys empires.

Your job as a strategist isn't to be perfect—it's to not be catastrophically stupid.

eighteen

# Reshaping the Market

Remove the rough edges,
and customers stop asking "why switch?"
They just switch. And once they do, they stay.

Markets are like restaurants. Customers walk in hungry—for convenience, for speed, for lower cost, for something that actually works. Most companies throw appetizers at them: a feature here, a discount there. Snacks. Customers nibble, but they're still hungry.

The real winners serve a full meal … *Come Hungry, Leave Full.*

Netflix didn't just rent DVDs—they killed late fees, then served up streaming at home, and eventually layered on original content as dessert. Apple didn't just make a smaller disc player—they put *1,000 songs in your pocket* and redefined portable music. Amazon didn't just sell books online—they made delivery frictionless, then redefined what "shopping" meant.

Reshaping the market isn't feeding a need in the moment. It's resetting the expectation of what a *"good meal"* looks like. Do that, and everyone else scrambles to rethink their menus—and most of them can't keep up.

Customers don't just remember who fed them. They remember who left them full and satisfied.

And here's the thing: everything we've covered so far has been how you set the table:

- **Chapter 13: CI as a Mindset.** You don't guess what people are hungry for, you see the battlefield and listen beyond what they say.
- **Chapter 14: CI as a Weapon.** You don't just feed customers —you starve competitors. Pricing, roadmaps, tempo— that's how you deny rivals their oxygen.
- **Chapter 15: Patterns.** Market shapers spot the faint signal before the crowd does. They recognize the second dolphin while everyone else is staring at the first one.
- **Chapter 16: Illusion of Insight.** They don't fall for the garnish—the pretty dashboard number or the overhyped claim—they interrogate assumptions until they know if it's real or noise.
- **Chapter 17: Signals, Noise, Timing.** Finally, they serve the meal at the right time. Not too early (fad), not too late (roadkill), but right in the sweet spot when the market's hungry and rivals are still fumbling with appetizers.

Now let's talk about how market shapers actually reshape the menu.

## Redefine Value—Change What "A Good Meal" Means

Most restaurants pile on side dishes. Safe. Easy. But great chefs rewrite the main dish, so you judge the plate by flavor, not filler.

Nespresso was an inside-out move—engineering convenience into capsules. Starbucks was an outside-in play—reading cultural shifts and turning coffee into a community.

- **Nespresso—Serve the Morning**
  While rivals obsessed over burr grinders and boiler pressure, Nespresso reframed value: barista-level espresso at home, one button, consistent every time. The conversation stopped being "Which grinder?" and became "How fast to coffee?" Convenience wasn't a bonus—it became the definition of premium.

**Change the taste so nothing else measures up.**

- **Starbucks—Own the Third Place** Traditional cafés used to be pit stops. Starbucks redefined them as rituals: not home, not work, but a *"third place."* Wi-Fi, comfy chairs, endless permutations, your name on the cup. It wasn't just coffee—it was identity and belonging.

Both reset the definition of *"good coffee"*:

**Nespresso =** quality x speed x consistency at home

**Starbucks =** experience x customization x status in public

Everyone else had to rewrite their menus—or get left behind.

**How to plate it so customers adopt your definition of "good":**

- Pick one North Star (time-to-value, reliability, ROI, community).
- Collapse complexity into consistency (presets, templates, "one-button" wins).

- Package the habit (subscriptions, loyalty, easy reorders).
- Kill garnish (features that don't drive the North Star).

Give them a repeatable line ("Barista at home, one button").

**Lesson:** Don't just make a better dish. Change the taste so nothing else measures up.

## Own the Choke Points—Control the Dining Room, Not Just the Kitchen

The best restaurants aren't just about food. They control who gets in, who gets served, and who keeps coming back.

In markets, choke points aren't recipes, they're gates: supply chains, distribution, customer access. Own those, and you don't just play the game—you dictate it.

### Costco—The Curated Kitchen

Costco isn't a buffet. It's a chef's tasting menu. Five winners instead of a hundred entrées. Each carefully curated for the taster/buyer. For suppliers, it's do-or-die: get on Costco's shelves and you're rich, get left out and you're invisible to 128 million hungry diners.

Then there's the cover charge—the membership fee. Costco flipped the dining model: customers pay just to get in the door. That one move funds the business, builds loyalty, and lets them price razor-thin while rivals scratch their heads.

### Sam's Club—The Buffet Line

Sam's tried to copy but ended up more buffet than curated kitchen: more dishes, less trust, no halo effect. Membership felt like Walmart with pallets, not a privilege.

**Lesson:** When you own the choke point, you don't compete in the market—you reshape it.

## Rewrite the Business Model ... Change How the Bill Works

Most restaurants charge by entrée. Clever chefs price the *experience*: tasting menus, wine pairings, memberships. The house wins, and guests feel smarter.

**Reset the appetite.**

### Spotify—All You Can Eat

Where others charged per track, Spotify flipped the bill: one flat subscription. Music went from ownership to utility. Changed how people thought about music consumption. The signal was faint, but Spotify saw it while others clung to the past.

### Amazon Prime—The Cover Charge

Free shipping became a membership. Bundle in perks: movies, music, groceries. Customers weren't buying products—they were buying into Amazon and its ecosystem.

### Uber Eats & DoorDash—Time on the Menu

They didn't sell more takeout; they sold time back. Customers paid for access and convenience; restaurants paid for demand they couldn't create. That's insight that passes the "So What?" test.

And it worked because both sides felt fed: customers got convenience, restaurants got revenue without more staff. That's the Golden Rule applied to business models: don't eat well while your diners leave hungry.

**Lesson:** Rewrite the bill and you don't just change how you get paid—you reset the appetite.

## Control the Tempo ... Run the Pass Like a Maestro

Every great kitchen has a pass—that little strip of counter where finished plates hit the line. The head chef runs the tempo. Too slow, diners complain. Too fast, dishes get sloppy. The magic is rhythm—running the pass like a maestro.

Markets work the same way. Customers don't just care *what* you serve; they care *when*. Winners set the tempo. They dictate the beat of launches and pivots—and make competitors play catch-up.

- **Nintendo Wii:** Underpowered console but launched at the right tempo. Affordable, family-friendly, perfectly timed for the casual gaming wave. They slowed down the arms race and sped up the mass market.
- **Tesla:** While automakers shipped features once a year, Tesla pushed over-the-air updates weekly. Customers learned to expect constant improvement. Competitors looked clumsy serving last year's meal and having to pay for today's.
- **Netflix:** Hollywood followed release calendars. Netflix dumped whole seasons at once. They didn't just serve meals—they set the binge rhythm the world now expects.

**Lesson:** Get the tempo right, and even average meals taste extraordinary.

### Erase Switching Friction ... Make It Easy to Become a Regular

The best restaurants don't just lure you in—they make sure you come back without thinking. The coat-check knows your name, the bartender remembers your drink, the bill splits cleanly. Zero friction.

Markets work the same way. The winners erase switching friction so becoming a "regular" feels effortless.

- **Shopify:** Before Shopify, setting up an online store was like cooking a ten-course meal blindfolded—domains, hosting, payment gateways, design. Shopify stripped away the pain: one platform, plug-and-play, and you're selling in hours. They turned thousands of small merchants into regulars by making the first bite effortless.
- **Zoom:** One link. No downloads. It just worked. While WebEx asked for plugins and passwords, Zoom asked for one click. In a pandemic, that wasn't convenience—it was survival.
- **Apple Pay:** Paying with your phone isn't a feature—it's the removal of friction. Tap, done. Once you've used it, going back to chip readers feels medieval.

**Lesson:** Remove the rough edges, and customers stop asking "why switch?" They just switch. And once they do, they stay.

## Change the Cuisine—Category Creators Rewrite the Menu

Category creators don't argue over appetizers. They don't fight on side dishes or discounts. They name the cuisine. Once you redefine the cuisine, every other restaurant looks dated.

### Salesforce—SaaS as a New Cuisine

In the early 2000s, Siebel, Oracle, and SAP kept stacking features like appetizers onto bloated entrées. Salesforce said: "*We don't even serve that food anymore.*" No Software. SaaS. Subscription pricing, fast deployment, browser access. Rivals were left hawking lasagna while customers lined up for sushi.

### Airbnb—More Room on the Plate

Hotels fought over points programs and breakfast buffets. Airbnb rewrote the cuisine: more space, more choice, often at lower cost. Entire homes instead of cramped rooms. Kitchens if you wanted them. Neighborhoods instead of tourist strips. The question stopped being *"Which hotel?"* and became *"Why hotel at all?"*

**Lesson:** Category creators don't serve better entrées. They open a new restaurant—and make the old menu irrelevant.

## Closing Note

Reshaping the market isn't about being a better cook. It's about redefining the taste, controlling the dining room, rewriting the bill, setting the tempo, removing friction, and—when you can—changing the cuisine entirely.

Do that, and you don't just win customers. You change what the market believes a good meal even is.

But here's the kicker: seeing the signals and reshaping the menu is only half the game. The other half is how you behave once you've set the table. Strategy lives or dies in the choices leaders make under pressure—the habits, instincts, and behaviors that either reinforce the edge or squander it.

That's where we go next: **strategic behavior.** Because even the best meal doesn't matter if you poison the dining room with the wrong conduct.

# key lessons

### 1. Don't Compete in the Market—Rewrite It Until Competitors Can't Play.

Reshape the taste. Own the dining room.

Rewrite the bill. Control the tempo.

Erase friction. Invent a new cuisine.

Do this, and you don't "win customers." You **reprogram what customers believe a good meal even is.**

### 2. Remove Friction Until It Feels Like Sliding Down a Well-Greased Waterslide.

Zoom beat WebEx because it didn't require a wizard, three plugins, and a blood sacrifice to join a meeting.

Shopify turned e-commerce from a 40-step nightmare into a weekend side hustle.

Apple Pay made plastic cards feel medieval.

If switching to your product doesn't feel effortless, customers won't switch.

If staying doesn't feel effortless, they won't stay.

### 3. Stop Serving Appetizers—Rewrite the Entire Damn Menu.

Most companies toss customers little feature-snacks and wonder why nobody's full.

Market shapers?

They drop a **full-course meal that resets expectations** and makes everyone else's offerings look like gas-station nachos.

Netflix killed late fees and torched Blockbuster.

Apple put a thousand songs in your pocket and buried the CD industry behind the dumpster.

If your product doesn't force competitors to rewrite their entire menu ... you're not reshaping the market—you're running a snack bar.

# part four

## Strategic Behavior

## Author's Note

# Strategic Behavior

Have you ever wondered why two equally smart people can start at the same place, but only one of them ends up thriving? Or why the person with the "right answer" so often gets ignored, while someone else, maybe with half the facts but twice the story, wins the room? Or why the boss you report to can shape your future more than the company on your résumé?

It's all about strategic behavior. And that's the messy reality of strategic behavior. It's not about markets or frameworks here. It's about people: you, your teams, your customers, even your rivals. And people don't always play by the rules.

Being technically right doesn't always move the ball forward—sometimes it just earns you enemies. A résumé without a clear differentiator can make you invisible. The wrong boss can drain not just your energy, but your health. Brilliant ideas can die on the vine if you can't communicate them in a way that makes people lean in. And culture—the invisible force shaping how words, gestures, and intentions are received—can easily trip you up faster than any competitor.

So how do you navigate all that?

The chapters within this section dig into those very challenges.

- You'll see what happens when you turn the CI lens inward and run a win-loss on yourself.
- You'll explore the difference between mentors who build you up and toxic ones who tear you down—and how to flip that experience into fuel.
- You'll learn how the Golden Rule isn't just moral advice, but a strategic filter, even a trapdoor, that can disarm rivals and build loyalty at the same time.

- You'll find out why raising five kids is the best management residency you never signed up for.
- You'll learn how humor can diffuse chaos in the moment.
- You'll discover why cultural fluency, not language fluency, is often the sharpest edge of all.

If the earlier parts of this book were about becoming strategic, staying strategic, and leveraging intelligence as a weapon, Part Four of *The UnConventional Strategist* is about living strategy in real time. It's the human side—where patience, empathy, grit, and curiosity become your real competitive advantage.

Because strategy isn't just what you think. It's how you show up.

nineteen

# CI for One ... Turning the Lens on Yourself

Experience is not a spectator sport.

Most people think competitive intelligence is just for companies. But here's the truth: **you** are in a market too. You've got competitors, blind spots, and hopefully, a differentiator. Every now and then, it's worth turning the CI lens inward.

I've done this. It's uncomfortable—like running a win-loss report on your career. But it works.

Ask:

- Who else is doing what I do—and doing it better?
- What are they learning, publishing, getting promoted for?
- Am I growing toward the market or clinging to relevance from 2016?

Then Red Team your résumé. Find someone you trust and let them poke holes in your narrative:

- "They've been doing the same thing for 5+ years."

- "No evidence of strategic impact."
- "Solid background—but forgettable."

If your résumé reads like a job description instead of a highlight reel, you've got work to do. If the feedback stings a little, good. That's the signal.

**CI isn't just how companies avoid irrelevance. It's how people do too.**

### The School of Hard Knocks: Learning the Hard Way

I hold multiple degrees from the School of Hard Knocks. Early in my career, I changed jobs frequently … trying to figure out what I liked, and didn't. Not exactly the fastest route to a decent paycheck or corner office, but it gave me perspective. Would I recommend it? Depends on your sense of "adventure."

I've told my kids, *"Find something you're passionate about and it won't feel like work."* Took seven years to realize that for me, it was product management—the role that let me flex and grow.

Getting there was a meandering journey.

Two of my childhood friends had it all mapped out: four years of college, advanced degrees, career trajectories set. John, a phenomenal trumpet player became an Emmy-winning photojournalist and has covered nearly every Denver Broncos game from the sidelines since 1985.

**Technically right, strategically lost.**

Me? I changed majors five times. Would've kept going if my parents hadn't cut me off. Crushed to learn there was no degree in "Undecided."

I ping-ponged from engineering to the College of Arts and Parties, then landed in business. Serendipity dropped me into a computer class—taught by a professor with a twisted sense of humor—that finally got me on track. It wasn't passion, but it was progress.

Somewhere along the line, I stopped asking, "What should I do?" and started asking, "Where can I create leverage?"

That shift mattered.

While I was figuring myself out, I noticed others pretending they had it figured out. Great résumés, zero self-awareness. Smart but tone-deaf. Technically right, strategically lost.

## Being Right vs. Being Successful

I've worked with people who always have to be right. You know the type. Being right feels good—smart, validated, seen. But it doesn't move the ball forward.

In fact, it can pull the team backward while the argument champion stands proudly atop a hill no one else wanted to climb. Everyone else just wants to play bar chess.

And then they wonder why they're sitting alone in the Tower of Isolation. They may have been right, but they weren't successful.

Trying to be always right is like pulling the pin on a grenade, dropping it down your pants, and then wondering what happened. Congrats, you've been nominated for a Darwin Award.

## Emotional Intelligence (EQ) Is Real

The root of "always right" syndrome? Low EQ. It often rides shotgun with technical brilliance and poor judgement. Like bleach and ammonia: useful alone, toxic when combined.

Robert Greene nails this in his *The 48 Laws of Power.* A king commissions a battering ram with specific measurements he wants. The builder delivers a technically superior version—not the one the king asked for. His reward for not following the king's order is execution. He was right—and dead.

Success beats being right. Successful people get invited back. Promoted. Trusted. As Mom used to say, pick your battles unless your goal is to piss off as many people as possible.

## Differentiate or Be Disposable

If you can't name your differentiator, you're probably competing on price, title, or tenure. That's a vulnerable place to be.

Ask yourself:

- What do I bring to the table that others in my role don't?
- What am I the go-to for?
- If my role disappeared tomorrow, what would people actually miss?

**In CI terms, you're a product—and generic products don't get premium positioning.**

## Life Is About Continuous Learning

One of the best CI moves you can make is *keep learning.*

I've worked across industries, geographies, and customer types. Knowing a little about a lot goes a long way.

**People with a hunger to learn will learn for themselves.**

Leil Lowndes' sage words in *How to Talk to Anyone* nails this: learn the lingo of many industries. Speaking someone's language creates instant connection.

And with today's generative AI tools, there's no excuse not to dive into a new space.

When I train salespeople, we role-play. I've played CIOs, CFOs, developers—even a CUO (Chief Underwriting Officer) at a fictional insurance firm. It forces you to think like them, speak like them, be them.

I've even presented at insurance industry conferences. Not because I came from the industry—but because I studied it enough over multiple years to appreciate what they do and challenges they face. This type of thinking influences what I look for in potential candidates for our team.

When people ask how I hire, I say this: I want people with insatiable curiosity, pattern recognition skills, ethical grounding, a great work ethic, and the ability to think past the obvious. Everything else can be taught.

People with a hunger to learn will learn for themselves. That trait is gold.

Just like in the studio: the mixing and fixing are never done.

Neither is self-improvement.

## Strategic Improv at Work—Lifetime of Learning

Experience
is not a spectator sport.

Early in my sales career, I inherited a brutal oil and gas account in the mid-'80s—right after the bust. It was the kind of market where bumper stickers begged, "Dear Lord, please let there be another oil boom and this time I promise not to piss it all away." Not exactly a buyer's paradise.

The account had a long, sour history with my company. Lucky me. The head of IT—let's just say he wasn't sending us holiday cards. I was young, ambitious, and clearly naïve. At our first meeting, it must have been apparent that beyond being able to spell "oil" and "gas," my industry knowledge was hovering somewhere close to zero.

I said I would like to spend some time with team to learn the business.

He looked at me—deadpan over his glasses—and dropped this:

**"I don't have any effing time to teach any effing vendor about my effing business."**

Nice opener, right? Basically the corporate version of spitting in your coffee when you asked for it black. No cream, thank you.

After the initial shock wore off (elapsed time: 21 seconds), I came back with:

**"Fine. I'll go learn about your effing business. Next time we meet, you can quiz me. If I pass, I get to talk to your staff."**

He blinked. "You'd actually do that?"

"Absolutely."

And I did. I dove in hard—studied upstream and downstream operations, primary, secondary, and tertiary recovery. Learned why a geologist views a seismic chart from the front while a geophysicist looks from the side. I understood how oil gets refined and why pump prices have nothing to do with what's in the ground. I even joined IEEE and AAPG (American Association of Petroleum Geologists), just to be fluent in their world.

I came back. Sat down with him. Took his quiz: 30 minutes of technical, operational, and strategic questions. I answered every one of them.

He didn't smile but he nodded. And he gave me access to his team.

We never became friends, but as I wrapped up that assignment, he gave me a parting gift:

"I still hate your company. But I respect you."

I'll take that any day. Because in business, especially in sales, access and respect aren't given. They're earned—through initiative, grit, and a willingness to outlearn everybody in the room.

## Empowering Others to Their Future

Once you've turned the CI lens inward, help others do the same. I've always believed part of a manager's job is to empower future versions of their team.

Whether it's technical skills, public speaking, executive communication, or just growing confidence—I invest in my team's learning.

Over three years, I sent more than 20 team members through competitive intelligence training. It took planning and budgeting, but the results spoke for themselves. They moved from tactical focus to strategic thinking.

They got better. Smarter. Sharper. So did our entire team.

## Close the Loop ... or Someone Else Will

Nobody's coming to hand you a strategy for your career. There's no quarterly roadmap review, no analyst report on your career trajectory. You are the product. And you're the strategist, the ops team, and marketing department.

That means it's on you to stay relevant, differentiated, and valuable. Because the moment you stop tuning your positioning, others will take your spot—and they won't send a calendar invite before they do, trust me.

## Lost in Translation—Abroad and Home

I went most of my life undiagnosed. As a kid, I jumbled words constantly: Wallduck store instead of Duckwalls. Mowlawner for lawn mower. Washing shamine. Pasgetti for Spaghetti. You get the idea. It wasn't until I was 21 or 22 that I realized—oh hey, I'm dyslexic.

I hated reading growing up. Especially those sadistic SRA color-coded booklets they made us plow through in school. Other kids devoured them like Skittles. I was stuck in burnt sienna while everyone else was sprinting into neon chartreuse.

To this day, Word's spell check and "Read Aloud" are my copilots.

College wasn't much better. Textbooks like *Organizational Design* felt like hieroglyphics. Yet oddly, I could read music and memorize it after a couple of read-throughs, note for note. I also found that dense legal books like the UCC (Uniform Commercial Code) strangely digestible. My brain made no sense … even to me.

For a long time, I lived in fear of being found out. That people would mock me. That I'd be dismissed as "slow" or "dumb." But I've since learned that dyslexia isn't rare. It shows up in execs, teammates, and friends. Some of the smartest people I know carry the same glitchy wiring.

I met Mike at my first job out of college. Early in my career, we bonded over Stephen King novels. One day he handed me *Dune* and said, "You've gotta read this." *Cue panic*. But I forced myself through it—and something clicked. What didn't make sense, is the story flowed off the pages. That one book helped me in starting to retrain my brain.

Now I read 20-25 books a year. Not because I have to. Because it helps me stay sharp. It keeps the dyslexia in check.

Eventually, I started opening up to people I trusted. I didn't share it as an excuse—more like a user manual.

## Is That Room 436 or 346?

I once worked for Greg—three times, actually. That's how much I trusted the guy. On a trip to Switzerland with him and our UK colleague Peter, Greg called my hotel room and said, "We're in Pete's room—436." But Peter looked confused: "We're in 346." Greg just grinned. "Don't worry, he's dyslexic. He'll figure it out."

A few minutes later, I knocked on their door. Laughter exploded on the other side. You see, Greg understood how my brain worked to his advantage.

It's your turn … turn the lens on yourself. Sharpen your edge. Learn what others won't.

Because whether you're leading a team or just trying to lead yourself, the game is the same:

**Evolve or be outpaced.**
**Adapt or be ignored. Improve or be replaced.**

# key lessons

### 1. If You Won't Analyze Yourself, the Market Will.

You **are** a product—with competitors, blind spots, and declining SKUs if you stop evolving.

Red-team your résumé. Audit your skills. If the truth stings? Good. That's your leading indicator.

### 2. Being "Right" Is Overrated—Being Effective Isn't.

People who always need to be right eventually end up **alone at the top of Mount Irrelevant.**

EQ beats IQ when it comes to promotions, influence, and not getting metaphorically executed like the guy in *48 Laws of Power.*

### 3. Differentiate, Learn Relentlessly, or Get Replaced.

If you can't articulate your differentiator, congratulations—you're the commodity option.

Your only defense is **continuous learning, insatiable curiosity, and the guts to out-study everyone else.**

Careers rot when people stop upgrading themselves.

twenty

# Be the Mentor You Wish You Had

Every successful leader has been fortunate to have someone who mentored, challenged, and looked after them.

In the television series *The Bear,* Jeremy Allen White's protagonist "Carmy" has a mentor and an antagonist he has to deal with. Chef Terry is Carmy's respected mentor and surrogate mother figure. She leads with compassion, artistry, and emphasis on human-centered hospitality. Chef Fields is Carmy's antagonist and tormentor who embodies everything toxic: cruel, dismissive, and psychologically scarring.

Veronica and I were watching an episode of this fantastic show, when it hit me … I've had my share of both. And unfortunately, my Chef Fields' outnumber the Chef Terrys about 7 to 1. That's not a great ratio.

I doubt I'm alone in that math. If you've been in the corporate world long enough, you've likely racked up a few of each. And while the bad ones teach you what not to do, it's the rare few—the

Chef Terrys—who quietly shape your trajectory, who model what leadership, trust, and generosity actually look like.

## Mentor Attributes That Work

This is my list. Yours might look different. But looking back at the best bosses who became my mentors, these are the common threads:

- **Real:** No corporate mask. No BS. Just authentic people you actually relate to.
- **Trustworthy:** I could tell them anything … and did.
- **Confident:** Secure enough to share their secrets, not guard them.
- **Empowering:** They let me run with it. Only rule? No surprises.
- **Fair:** They listened. Didn't always agree, but always gave a fair shake.
- **Guiding:** Offered advice with no hidden agenda.
- **Empathetic:** Took the time to understand where I was coming from.
- **Protective:** Always had my six.
- **Honest:** Gave it to me straight: feedback, direction, the hard stuff.
- **Human:** Could laugh with me. Could laugh at themselves.
- **No micromanaging:** They trusted me to do the job they hired me for.

I don't need to list the other kind—you've probably work for a few. Arrogant. Controlling. Toxic. You know the type.

## Choose Your Boss Carefully

Rishad Tobaccowala, author of *Rethinking Work,* nailed it in his blog *"Career Lessons Revisited"* when he wrote:

**"Who you work for is critical so choose your boss well," and "The key to success is to find and hold on to the right boss."**

He doesn't stop there:

> A successful boss … makes new opportunities for you, but also ensures they have your back while being very upfront and straightforward with you face to face. They challenge you but cover for you when necessary. Find one or more of these and hold on tight. It makes all the difference and every successful leader has been fortunate to have someone who mentored, challenged, and looked after them.

I've had a few like that. Greg, my Bar Chess partner for one—I worked for him more than once. He wasn't the only great boss I had, but he had the most impact on my career and life.

And then there were the others—the ones I wish I had never worked for. Plenty of them.

So what do you do when you land under a toxic boss? The answer depends on your glass.

If you're a half-empty kind of person, you may grit your teeth, keep your head down, and try to survive. I did that once—stuck it out to protect my team. But the cost was pretty steep—my health took a hit … mentally and physically. And the truth is, I should've walked. No job is worth that much damage. Another degree earned. Sigh.

If you're a half-full type, you might see it differently. You'll see it as a sign. A prompt to explore what's next. Because whatever's next has got to be better than staying stuck under someone who drains the life out of you.

By the way, everyone should read Rishad's blog. It's packed with wisdom and experience no matter where you are in your journey.

## Surviving a Toxic Boss When You Can't Escape

From others who have been in similar situations, I've created collective lessons to use if you ever find yourself under the boot of a power-hungry micromanager, these might help:

**Build skills while you're in the fire.**

- **Document everything:** Approvals, conversations, commitments—save it. It's your personal insurance policy.
- **Talk to HR, but do it strategically:** You don't need to file a complaint. Sometimes a casual "this new manager could use some professional coaching" is enough to flag it—and protect yourself if things escalate.
- **Don't internalize the chaos:** Boss' dysfunction isn't your fault. See the behavior for what it is. Not a reflection of you, but a pattern of how they handle everything.
- **Build skills while you're in the fire:** Treat this as a real-time case study in leadership failure. Learn from it what not to do.
- **Explore your exit:** If the writing's on the wall, ask for a voluntary separation package. Better to walk with dignity (and severance) than stick around and suffer.

A toxic boss teaches you something too—if only by contrast. Once you've survived one, you realize just how powerful the *opposite* can be.

So instead of repeating the cycle, flip it.

Be the mentor you wish you had.

## Be the Mentor You Wish You Had ... and Others Will Desire

**Great mentors create more mentors.**

No black magic required. Being a great mentor is mostly about being the kind of person you wish you'd had guiding you. Here's how:

- **Listen more than you talk:** Ask thoughtful questions. Be curious, not just corrective.
- **Give value—add advice:** Real, practical, insightful advice. Help them navigate those murky waters.
- **Be authentic:** People can smell performance a mile away. Don't fake it.
- **Explain the why:** Share the context behind them.
- **Invest in their growth:** Help them get better, not just get things done.
- **Have their back:** Especially when they're not in the room.

Mentorship isn't a title—it's a mindset. But if you're already leading, start thinking of "mentor" as one of your most important job descriptions. If you're not in management yet, mentoring someone else is the best prep you'll ever get.

It's also how you change the system. Great mentors create more mentors. That's how you pay it forward.

You don't need a title to be a mentor. You just need to give a damn. When you do that, watch what happens to the people around you.

## The Persistent Son-of-a-Bitch

Looking back, my first mentors didn't carry that label. They were parents, coaches, teachers, Scoutmasters … individuals who shaped me before I knew what mentorship even was.

But my first real mentor, the one who stuck, was Roger. He was VP of IT at a well-known media giant and gave a talk at our college tech club, a thinly disguised Friday Afternoon Club (FAC). Afterwards, I asked him for an internship.

His answer: "We don't hire interns. But keep in touch."

So I did. Every month.

Same response. Month after month. Until my seventh attempt, when he finally gave in and handed me a role testing Lotus 1-2-3 for a corporate project. I asked him what changed. His answer?

"You're a persistent son-of-a-bitch."

Roger became more than a mentor—he became a career-long advisor and lifelong friend. He taught me how to navigate the business world before I'd even graduated. When it came time to get a real job, he didn't offer me one. He pointed me to a company that would grow me faster … and he was right.

## Pay It Forward … Then Get Out of the Way

I tell every young person on my team the same thing: just promise me that when I get old, you'll hire me to wash the dishes.

One of my brightest team members was a young, ambitious guy with a strong work ethic—and an accent that made him stand out, not back. He asked me how to prep for his next role. I told him:

go on as many interviews as you can. Learn the questions. Practice the answers. That's how you get good and develop that muscle.

One Friday night, I got a voicemail that sounded like one of my kids when they wrecked the car: "Hey, Jay … can you call me?"

Turns out, he'd landed an offer at a competitor. Better money. Better title. He wanted to talk it through. I didn't hesitate: "If you don't take it, I'll come out there and introduce your rear to the tip of my shoe."

Being a mentor or manager isn't about keeping people. It's about launching them. That's the job. And when they fly, it's just as rewarding as any promotion you'll ever get. He's out there crushing it now, and I couldn't be prouder.

## The Ripple Effect Is Real

I mentored a team member who co-managed the team with me and then I promoted to be my peer. Team members commented that his style and approach was so similar to mine, they couldn't tell us apart. Twin sons of different mothers.

**Good mentorship has downstream impact.
You don't always see it, but it multiplies.**

Mentorship doesn't end when your mentee leave the company. It echoes. They carry what you taught them—how you treated them, what you modeled—into their next job, their next team, and maybe their own mentees.

You want a real legacy? It's not your title. It's the people you launched who are now launching theirs.

You don't need a plaque or a promotion to leave a legacy. The people who carry your advice, your belief in them, your examples. That's legacy.

Remember that 7:1 ratio at the beginning of this chapter? Your mission is to flip it around. You get to decide what ratio you'll leave behind. Will you be somebody's Chef Terry? Will you be the one they name years from now when someone asks, "Who helped you the most?"

You don't need a team to be that person. Just a decision. A question. A nudge. A hand on someone's back when they need it most.

# key lessons

### 1. Flip the Ratio: Be the Mentor Someone Names 20 Years From Now.

The world has enough tyrants, micromanagers, and insecure bosses with fragile egos and big titles. Your job?

**Increase the number of Chef Terrys in circulation.** Become the one people talk about when asked, "Who changed everything for you?"

### 2. Your Legacy Isn't Your Title— It's the Army of People You Helped Become Better Than You.

Promotions fade. Org charts disappear.

But the people you coached? They carry your fingerprints into every job they touch.

That's the ripple effect.

That's the real inheritance you leave behind.

### 3. Mentorship Isn't Management. It's Impact, Legacy, and Sometimes Saving Someone's Career.

A real mentor:

- listens
- protects
- challenges
- invests
- tells you the hard truth
- gets out of the way when it's your time to fly

Be that person. Launch people. Shove them toward better futures.

If they surpass you? Even better. That means you did it right!

twenty one

# The Golden Rule ... Strategy at Work

You didn't even sell us the product.
But you owned the problem.
That's why we trust you.

What if the softest skill you learned in kindergarten was your sharpest edge in business?

Sounds soft? It's not.

It's pattern recognition. It's strategic empathy. It's understanding what motivates people—what they need, what they fear, how they act when no one's watching. And in business, that's power.

## The Golden Rule Is a Pattern Too

Reciprocity is a behavior signal. When people feel seen, respected, and supported, they tend to give more: information, trust, commitment. I've found this applies everywhere: teammates, customers, even competitors.

You can learn a lot just by watching how people treat others. That tells you how they expect to be treated. It also tells you about the culture behind them. Are they dismissive or collaborative?

Calculated or authentic? Guarded or generous? The same's true across global cultures—how someone treats you often mirrors how they expect to be treated.

Let me tell you about "Larry."

Larry barked orders, crushed deadlines, and torched people in meetings—full dragon mode. I figured he was wired that way.

I talked with one of his direct reports who said—dead serious —"Larry's actually the nicest guy on the planet."

Planet.

I thought he was joking. Turns out, Larry would put on a *persona*. Aggressive to outsiders, supportive inside his team. Not my style, but once we grabbed a coffee and I saw the real guy, I understood his motives. He was playing a role. Strategic? Maybe. Intentional for sure. And he really *is* a nice guy.

Point: behaviors are patterns too. You can miss the signal if you only look at what's loud.

## Using the Golden Rule with Customers

Everyone talks about "customer obsession." Most of it's performative.

Here's how you earn trust: show up. Communicate. Don't vanish when things go sideways.

We had just acquired a small company when one of their big financial customers hit the wall. Chaos. The problem was impacting their business in a bad way. I promised I'd call them twice a day, 11:00 a.m. and 4:00 p.m., until it was fixed. Even if the update was: "Still working on it."

**The Golden Rule doesn't make you soft.**

I was exhausted and, on the road, but kept my word. Twice a day. Everyday. Persistence.

Two weeks later, we fixed it. A few months later, they signed a massive order with us. Not because the product was perfect, but because we treated them like valued customers.

Their quote stuck with me: "You didn't even sell us the product, but you owned the problem. That's why we trust you."

That's how you earn trust. Not with noise. With follow-through.

## The Golden Rule as a Manager

When I first took over the CI team, we were four people and a folding table.

I told them:

**"I'll never ask you to do something I wouldn't do myself."**

And I meant it. I gave them five Golden Rules:

1. I'll treat you how I'd want to be treated.
2. I'll treat you as a peer, not a pawn.
3. I won't micromanage you. Ask for help if you need it.
4. I'll respect your time, your talent, your ideas.
5. I'll give advice, not orders. What you do with it is your call.

Fifteen years later, with teams that've grown beyond 20 people, I still work this way.

**Performance:** Top tier.

**Turnover:** Almost zero.

**Trust:** Earned.

I treat my team like people, not resources. I try to lead, not manage. If they're open to it, I learn about their lives—families, hobbies, what drives them. When life gets messy—illness, grief, burnout—I ask myself, *"How would I want to be treated right now?"* Then I lead with that.

The Golden Rule doesn't make you soft. It builds loyalty … and there's nothing soft about that.

## When It Comes to Competitors …

I don't trash-talk competitors. Not because I'm polite—because it muddies strategy.

I treat them like a worthy chess opponent: eyes open, respect intact, assumptions low. I channel my inner Musashi—no emotion, no ego, no shortcuts.

**Trash-talking isn't strength.**

Once, I was speaking at a conference. The presenters before me were all competitors. Each took a turn slinging mud, freely disparaging competitors. It was awkward. The "air" in the room felt disjointed, not good. The audience wasn't buying it.

When I got up, I said:

**"I'm not here to talk about the other companies and their products. I'm only here to talk about how we solve your problems."**

Applause. Instantly.

Because here's the truth: trash-talking isn't strength. It's insecurity with a mic. It signals weak product, reactive culture, and a team that lead with emotion instead of intelligence.

Not a company I'd trust. Definitely not one I'd follow.

## The Golden Rule Strategic Filter

If you want to use the Golden Rule as a competitive advantage, here's a simple test I've used for years involving the companies and people I work with:

- **People:** How would I want to be treated in this situation?
- **Teams:** What kind of manager would I want to work for?
- **Competitors:** How can I compete without contempt and still win?

These three questions keep your judgment sharp, and your strategy grounded. They help you lead with clarity instead of ego.

**Use the Golden Rule as a Strategic Filter.**

## The Competitive Intelligence Trapdoor

Here's the secret most people miss: being respectful isn't just decent. It's strategic. Especially when your competitor's a jerk.

**The goal isn't to win the argument.**

When people don't see you as a threat, they get sloppy. They posture. They reveal too much. They get emotional instead of analytical. That's when they start showing you their cards. They brag.

I've learned more in one cordial dinner, on an airplane seat, bar, or restroom with a loudmouth competitor than in a dozen win-loss reports. Because while they're busy flexing, I'm watching. I'm listening. I' m connecting dots. And I'm figuring out what they don't think I'll pick up on. That's the Golden Rule, weaponized as a trapdoor. They won't even see it. But you will. And your outcomes will reflect it.

Surprisingly, people underestimate you when you're respectful and curious. Good. Let them. That's when they start showing their hand.

The goal isn't to win the argument. It's to win the market. Let them underestimate you. While they're posturing, you're planning your move.

### Playing the Long Game

Play short games, win short. Play long, win big.

That means every interaction with customers, partners, even your competitors is a chance to build your reputation, not just hit your quota.

People remember how you show up when it's hard. How you act when the deal's slipping. How you respond when they choose someone else. Burn the bridge or build a longer one?

I once lost a deal to a competitor and still congratulated the customer on their decision. Not sarcastically. Genuinely. I said, "If that's best for your business now, I respect it. I'll be here if anything changes."

Eighteen months later, guess who they called? Not the competitor.

Sometimes the real advantage isn't how you win. No, it's how you lose. *And what you do next.*

That's the long game. And few play it.

## Applying the Filter

Use the Golden Rule as a litmus test for decisions … for you personally, for the team, the product, your customer, or go-to-market. Use it everywhere.

When in doubt, ask: *Would I want to be on the receiving end of this?* If the answer's no, it should guide your actions.

Would I want to use this product? Hear this message? Sit through this call? Follow this leader?

If the answer's no: fix it.

The Golden Rule isn't just a moral compass. It's a strategic shortcut to customer experience, employee trust, and market alignment.

**Using the Golden Rule doesn't require permission.**

### Not Soft. Sharp.

The Golden Rule sounds gentle. But it's not.

- It's focused.
- It's intentional.
- It's dangerous to underestimate.

People perform better when they're respected. Customers stay longer when they're treated like partners. Competitors slip up when you treat them with quiet, disarming respect.

This isn't moral fluff. It's strategic pressure applied with precision.

And absolutely critical when you're operating in other cultures. It helps provide the confidence needed when communicating with peers, customers, and executives.

## What About When They Don't Deserve It

Not everyone earns your respect. But that's not the point.

The Golden Rule isn't about fairness. It's about leverage.

I've dealt with aggressive execs, difficult partners, even hostile competitors. And the people around me watched how I handled it. Calm. Focused. Professional.

That's how you build your brand.

It works even when it's not returned. Because someone's always watching.

The Golden Rule doesn't require permission. It requires perspective. Power doesn't always raise its voice.

# key lessons

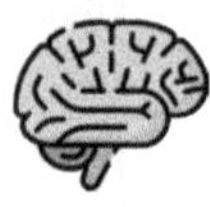

**1. The Golden Rule Isn't Kindness—It's Leadership.**

Treat people the way you want to be treated, and they instinctively mirror it:

- more openness
- more honesty
- more signal
- more access

It's about being human and a leader. Even in discipline, apply it with love and genuinely wanting to help the person to improve. That's the difference between a leader or being the south-end of a north-bound horse.

**2. Reliability Beats Performance—Be the One That Shows Up Consistently.**

You didn't win that financial customer because your product was flawless.

You won because you **showed up twice a day for two weeks while the world was on fire.**

In a market filled with vendors who disappear the moment something breaks, steady communication is a killer advantage.

Want irrational customer loyalty?

Be the only adult in the room when things get ugly.

**3. The Long Game Rewards People Who Don't Set Fires.**

Lose a deal?

Congratulate the customer sincerely.

You're playing chess, not whack-a-mole.

Eighteen months later, they called you back—*because you played like a professional, not a pyromaniac.*

Short-game people win quarters. Long-game people win markets.

twenty two

# How to Not Suck at Public Speaking ... or at least, Avoid Getting Booed

Public speaking isn't some magical birthright.

Let me take you back to my first public speaking class, aka the seventh circle of hell for introverts. The instructor started things off with this cheery nugget, "There are only two things people fear more than anything: public speaking and death." And honestly, after my first presentation, death didn't sound so bad.

Being a great strategist doesn't matter if no one hears you. And no one will hear you if you suck at speaking. Want influence? You better learn how to show up, speak up, and not bore the room to death.

I hated that class. Or maybe I hated the audience. Hard to say. Standing in front of my peers—who, let's be honest, were mostly rooting for me to trip on my own shoelaces. I had to present something I didn't care about to people who didn't care either. And to make it even more excruciating, we were videotaped. Yes, I got to watch myself nervously fig-leafing my hands over my crotch, or doing that awkward "butt-lift" stance like I was prepping to bow at a royal dinner. Then came the steepling, the aimless pacing, jingling of coins with hands in pockets, and, of course, the classic fallback: "um."

**There is no substitute for doing IT.**

Humiliating doesn't even cover it. But it was also oddly motivating. Even for an introvert like me.

Once my ego bruises healed, I made a decision: I was going to get good at this. Not TED Talk good, but at least not get-laughed-out-of-the-room bad. I actually listened to the instructor, tried the exercises, and by the end of the course—four days later—I was noticeably better. Like "holy crap, is that the same guy?" better. The transformation gave me enough confidence to keep working on it.

The real breakthrough came when I stopped thinking of public speaking as *speaking* and started thinking of it as *storytelling*. The best speakers aren't just knowledgeable. They're entertaining. They're relatable. They make you feel something—even if it's just, "Thank God it's not me up there." Whether they're talking about leading a team through chaos or just explaining how to fix a broken toilet, they *tell a damn good story*.

I say this elsewhere in the book, and I'll say it again here: there is no substitute for doing IT. You can learn the theory, but unless you're actually standing in front of a room full of people, you'll never build the conviction—this means real people, not your dog or mirror. Same goes for managing people. Or selling. You can't fake confidence. You either have it, or your audience's crossed arms and glazed-over eyes will let you know you don't. Ugh.

And trust me, they're not subtle about it.

Maybe it's because I'm a musician as well, but public speaking never rattled my nerves. To me it was just another form of performance in front of an audience.

## The Myth of Natural Talent: Why Great Speakers Are Made, Not Born

Yes, there are people who seem to be born with it. Charisma just oozes out of them. They flash a smile, raise an eyebrow, and suddenly they've got the room eating out of their hand like a snake charmer hypnotizing a cobra.

And then there are the others. You know the type ... verbal freight trains with no brakes. Full speed into a presentation and never quite sure when, or how, to stop. Diarrhea of the mouth with no Imodium in sight. The audience leaves more exhausted than enlightened.

And let's not forget our friend, "mumbles." Lulls the audience into a stupor in 90 seconds flat.

Assuming you're somewhere in the middle—an average Jane or Jay like me, here's the real secret: public speaking isn't some magical birthright. It's a skill. A craft. A muscle you can train. You just need the right mix of mechanics, confidence, and good ol' fashioned self-awareness.

## Be Authentic, but Not a Mess

The best speakers aren't the slickest. They're the most *authentic*. People can smell fake a mile away, and nobody enjoys being marketed to by a cardboard cutout. Be real. Be you. Just the slightly elevated, more intentional version of you, with fewer filler words and more purpose behind your gestures.

And yes, sprinkle in some fun. People don't want to be lectured to; they want to feel something. Inspired. Entertained. Or at the very least, not bored stiff.

## The Eyebrow Test

How do you know if you're connecting? Watch their eyebrows. Raised = interested. Furrowed = confused … or maybe your fly is down. Flat = you lost them. Move on.

One trick I swear by: **work the room with your eyes.** Pick out actual people—row by row and at different locations—and speak to them. Not in a creepy "I see you" way, but in a "you matter and I'm including you in this moment" kind of way. If the room is big, like at a conference, even a glance in someone's general direction can make half the row think you're speaking just to them.

I once spoke at an industry conference in Waltham, Massachusetts. The room was packed with over 2,000 people waiting for the big rollout. I was the product manager, so naturally I got the glamorous job of introducing the product to the crowd. I used all the tricks: authenticity, eye contact, a touch of humor, and a clear message. Afterward, people came up and said, "It felt like you were speaking *just to me.*" I ended up chatting with folks for 90 minutes post-talk. Honestly, it felt more like a great gig than a presentation.

## Every Gig Is a Rehearsal

Every presentation is a chance to test, learn, and tweak. What landed? What flopped? What did you do out of habit that you should probably retire (looking at you, pacing-in-a-circle guy)?

Everything on stage should be intentional. Think voice, volume, pacing, movement, and gestures. Are you walking across the stage because it makes sense in the story ... or are you just trying to get your steps in?

That's what make the TED Talks so great. It has a very specific formula and time boundaries to it. It has guidelines for that 18 minute, or less, talk. It forces you to create a message, stay on message, and make your presentation impactful. Even without using GenAI.

## Laughter: The Secret Weapon ... or the Fastest Way to Die on Stage

Lastly, let's talk about humor. Americans love to kick off a presentation with a joke, like it's required by law. And when it lands, great. You've set a tone, built rapport, and loosened the room.

But when it doesn't? You can practically hear the *thud* as it hits the floor, right next to your credibility. I've watched speakers deliver a joke in Europe or Asia that works back home in the US, only to be met with silence colder than a Minnesota January.

So, here's the golden rule: **Know. Your. Audience.**

## Humor Rules of Engagement:

- **Self-deprecating humor?** Usually safe. It shows humility.
- **Political jokes?** Don't. Just don't.
- **Cultural references?** Unless you're *sure* they'll get it, skip it.
- **Humor as seasoning, not sauce.** Think garnish, not gravy. You're not doing standup; you're building connection.

If you must attempt humor, at least have the **emotional intelligence** to know when to pull the ripcord. If the first laugh doesn't come, don't double down. Move on. Quickly. Now.

Some ways to evaluate whether to say it or not:

- Would I say this to my boss?
- Would I say this in front of my mom?
- Would I be okay seeing this quote all over the internet the next day?

If it fails one of those you might just want to keep it in your back pocket. Or throw it away.

## Why This All Matters: Speak Well or Be Forgotten

So why go through the pain of learning to speak in public? Why deal with the nerves, the awkward silences, the risk of your voice cracking like a teenager in a school play?

Because being able to clearly, confidently, and convincingly communicate your ideas is **a superpower.** It's what separates the people who *do great work* from the people who get *noticed* for doing great work.

Be honest with yourself: the world isn't always a meritocracy. You can be the smartest person in the room, but if you can't explain your ideas to others with clarity … or worse, if you bore them to death while trying … don't be surprised when someone else with half your brains and twice your polish gets the gig, the funding, or the promotion.

**It's about finding your voice.**

## The Benefits ... a.k.a. Why You Should Care

- **Career Growth**
  Strong speakers get noticed. They get invited to the meetings that matter, and sometimes, they're even asked to lead them. Weird, right?

- **Influence**

  Whether you're pitching an idea, selling a product, or convincing your kid to eat broccoli, the ability to persuade is everything.

- **Credibility**

  Sounding confident makes people *believe* you're competent. This is the dangerous truth that mediocre people have been using for centuries.

- **Leadership Presence**

  No one ever said, "Wow, I really respect how Jay read those bullet points verbatim." Command the room, or someone else will.

- **Personal Growth**

  It's not just about the spotlight. It's about finding your voice. Speaking well forces you to think clearly, prepare intentionally, and be fully present in the moment. It's therapy with a mic.

## The Final Word ... Before You Drop the Mic

You don't have to be the funniest, flashiest, or most charismatic person in the room. You just have to be real, be clear, and care enough to improve. That alone puts you ahead of 90% of the corporate karaoke acts out there reciting slides with the energy of a houseplant.

Public speaking is a skill anyone can build. And once you do, you'll find it opens more doors, earns more respect, and connects you with more people than just about anything else you can learn.

Next time you're asked to present, don't fake a cough or disappear quietly. Step up. Speak like it matters—because it does. You're not just sharing slides. You're showing who you are. And done right, you'll make someone out there think: "Damn … I want to do that too."

# key lessons

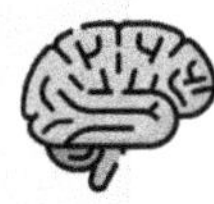

### 1. Storytelling Beats Slides ... Every Single Time.

Facts inform.

Slides support.

But *stories* make people care.

The best speakers aren't performing speeches—they're taking the audience on a journey with clarity, pacing, humor, and emotional beats.

If your audience doesn't feel something, they won't remember anything.

### 2. Connection Is the Real Metric ... Watch Their Eyebrows.

Public speaking is a two-way channel:

- Raised brows → you've got them.
- Furrowed → you lost them or confused them.
- Flat → you bored them into a light coma.

Use eye contact, presence, and intentional movement to wake the room back up and bring them with you.

**Attention is earned, not assumed.**

### 3. Speak Like It Matters: Because It Does.

You can be brilliant, but if you can't communicate that brilliance, someone else will outshine you with half the insight and twice the confidence.

Public speaking is the difference between being **heard** and being **ignored** ... between doing great work ... and being known for it.

twenty three

# Peerceptions, Politics, and the "Lazy American" Myth

Language is slippery,
and assumptions are dangerous.

Yes, your eyes read the chapter title right. "Peerceptions" is misspelled on purpose. English is my first language.

But if you've ever worked internationally, you've seen it first hand: how myths, assumptions, and half-truths shape how entire cultures perceive each other. And if you're smart, you learn to play those perceptions to your advantage.

This chapter isn't just about Japan. It's about image vs. reality, the strategic power of perception, and why being underestimated is sometimes your best move.

## Sakurauchi and the Bullshit Bias

It's a foggy April night, and I'm thinking back to Tokyo in the late '80s and early '90s. Specifically, January 1992 when Yoshio Sakurauchi, a Japanese politician—read: blowhard—declared that "lazy Americans" couldn't compete with Japan.

I took offense. So did others and it kicked off a "buy American" backlash. I wrote a scathing rebuttal in a local paper, which didn't exactly thrill my employer. But Sakurauchi had it coming. Less than two years later, Japan's economy hit the wall while the "lazy" US kept humming along as Japan slid into "The Lost Decade." This, of course, after they went on a buying spree, scooping up Columbia Pictures, Rockefeller Center, and half of America's commercial real estate portfolio.

God has a wicked sense of irony.

On the ground in Tokyo between 1990 and 1992, it was obvious the shine was fading. Japan's reputation for discipline and economic supremacy was built on their own mythology, not sustainability. The reality? A society that was socially exhausted, not financially poor.

**Behind the curtain, the cracks were visible.**

Think: the "salaryman" who clocked in at 5 a.m., clocked out at 2 a.m., and crashed in a coffin-sized capsule before repeating the cycle. People were routinely going to the hospital for exhaustion.

Fiction? Absolutely not. I observed it myself working over there.

## Detroit vs. Tokyo ... Lifestyle as a Strategy

I learned to separate the Japanese people … definitely wonderful from the politicians, still awful. And after living in Detroit around the same time—that's pronounced "Day-Twah" for my Canadian friends—I saw the other side. Japanese auto execs and managers in Detroit struggled with the idea of being repatriated back to Japan.

Why?

Because they got a taste of something dangerous: balance. Family dinners. Weekends off. Time to breathe. No nightly liver torture.

Let's break down the mythology. The Japanese "salaryman" was idolized as the engine of Japan's late-'80s boom. Long hours. Total dedication. National pride. But behind the curtain, the cracks were visible.

Here's what a "typical" workday actually looked like as I experienced it. Like everything in life, "mileage will vary" and others may have different experiences. This was my observation:

- **9:00:** Arrive, hungover. Chitchat.
- **10:00:** Call equally hungover customers to confirm meetings.
- **11:00:** More chitchat.
- **11:30:** Lunch.
- **12:30:** Head out for client meetings.
- **1:00:** First customer meeting.
- **2:00:** Travel to second meeting.
- **3:00:** Second meeting.
- **4:00:** Head back toward office … not to the office.
- **5:00:** Stop at pachinko parlor.
- **6:00:** Return to office.
- **7:00:** Instant noodles, phone calls, bullshitting.
- **8:00:** Quick sync with boss.
- **9:00:** Wrap up. Maybe.
- **10:00:** Head to bar for 3–5 hours of "team bonding" … i.e., drinking like it's a job.

Plenty of hours. Mistook *activity* for *productivity*. The Mandela Effect at work and an entire nation believing its own overhyped press releases.

I asked a guy in the office why he didn't just finish and go home. His answer was quick, "I can't. The neighbors would talk terribly about me and call me lazy." Self-inflicted wounds at a national level. Talk about a status quo.

## Better to Be the Gaijin

As a third generation American of Japanese descent, I am a *Sansei.* It means I am a grandchild of Japanese immigrants. I wanted to connect with my roots. Learning the language wasn't a completely heavy lift since I learned some as a child.

One day I gave a cabbie directions in Japanese. He fired something back. I told him to slow down—not the car, his words. "I'm American," I said.

He raised his eyebrows. "Ehh?" was his response. His "ehh" was Japanese for WTF. "I thought you were native. No accent!"

No accent and communicating in Japanese. That … became a problem.

Being underestimated was a strategic edge.

You see, being a Sansei, speaking Japanese, understanding Japanese, eating the native food, led my boss to expect me to *behave* Japanese. I could hear *The Vapors* singing *Turning Japanese* in the background.

Nope. I wasn't going to shuffle my feet or be deferential. I didn't bow deeply. I asked direct questions in meetings.

Eventually, I learned the secret: **lean into being the dumb Gaijin.** Gaijin is a Japanese word for a foreigner in Japan. Expectations dropped. Friction disappeared. I got more done. Being underestimated was a strategic edge.

## It's Groovy, but Not Helpful

Of course, I had to unlearn a few things too. Especially the language my grandparents brought over in the 1890s.

I'd use words like *benjo* for toilet. Today it's *toi-re*. People looked at me like I was quoting Shakespeare.

It's like a Millennial saying, "That's groovy." Sure, I understand it. But … why?

Language evolves. Culture evolves. But perception, especially outdated, romanticized perception, sticks like gum on a shoe.

## Yes Means No

Anyone who's spent more than five minutes abroad knows we're all bound by our cultural biases. Breaking news: so is everyone else.

I spent over two years bouncing between Pittsburgh—yes, it has its own dialect—and Tokyo, mostly in the Shinjuku area. Pittsburgh is a fantastic city with great people, and by the way, has quirky expressions like *gumbands, goin' aht, jeetjet?*, and *gyntegyl*. If you know, you know.

**The problem isn't content … it's the *context*.**

But let's focus on Japan.

In Japanese culture, you almost never hear the word *"no."* Instead, you'll hear *"yes"*… which actually means *"no."* Why? Because *"no"* is not socially acceptable in their polite society. Remember how it sounded when you asked your dad to borrow the car? You get the picture.

Here's how it works.

You make a request. They smile, nod politely, and say, *"Yes."* Then you wait. And follow up. And they smile again. And say yes again. After trying 100 different phrasings, you finally ask, "So… are you saying you don't have this item?"

They smile and beam. "Yes, that is correct." The point is that *you* had to figure it out.

Is it changing? Sure. Japanese Millennials and Gen Zers are slowly updating the playbook. But culture evolves at the speed of bureaucracy. Don't hold your breath.

If you want a laugh-out-loud book that gets the whole Japan/US culture clash right, find a used copy of *Japan: It's Not All Raw Fish* by Don Maloney. It's out of print, but you can still snag one for under $15 on Amazon. Worth every Yen.

## Are You Confused? I Am.

Language brings its own special kind of chaos. Especially when we toss around colloquialisms without a second thought … like saying, "I need a vanilla Windows configuration." What?

Now, translate that literally. Somewhere in Tokyo, a confused engineer is wondering what ice cream has to do with operating systems.

The problem isn't content … it's the **context.**

If you're a product manager with global customers, take this seriously. Translation isn't just about swapping English for Japanese or any other language. It's about **local usage, cultural interpretation, and intent.** That applies to everything from user manuals to product menus to how your US choices land with customers overseas.

And even if you've personally slaved over the translated documentation, guess what? It's probably still wrong.

The only way to get it right? Have a native speaker or translator, in that country, do it for you. Let them argue among themselves. It's not worth the headache even if it is a noble cause. Anything else is just … lost in translation.

## Colloquialisms Are Age and Culturally Relevant

Let's face it. Phrases used by Boomers—I'm guilty here—aren't the same ones Millennials or Gen Zers use. And vice versa.

Want to confuse a Millennial? Casually ask: *"Is it bigger than a breadbox?"* and watch their face go into full buffering mode as System 2—thanks, Daniel Kahneman—tries to parse what the hell you just said.

**Languages evolve just like people and cultures.**

A few classics:

- Once in a blue moon
- Beyond the pale
- Wall Street
- Cat's got your tongue?
- Rarer than hen's teeth

My personal favorites? *Beyond the pale and Wall Street.* Here's a fun bit of etymology: When New York was first settled, a literal wall was built to protect early colonists. That wall's long gone, but the name stuck: Wall Street. Going "beyond Wall Street" meant going "beyond the pale" … look that one up, it's got layers.

And no, Grandpa, **WTF** does not mean "Where's The Food."

Even my wife's bestie—fluent in her German parents' dialect—gets corrected by cousins in Germany. Turns out languages evolve just like people and cultures. It's life.

## Badly Lost in Translation

When I was a kid, we didn't travel much. But one trip stands out: flying to Los Angeles, visiting Disneyland, Japantown, the Carnation milk factory, and the La Brea Tar Pits.

In Japantown, we ate at a favorite, the Atomic Café that served incredible traditional Japanese food beside sushi. It's now long gone. Later, I  learned it was owned by a distant relative of my aunt's husband. That trip was the first time I really started to appreciate my heritage.

I also saw my first L.A. Dodgers game, thanks to my dad's friend, Charles, a second generation Nisei. It was at that game that he shared a story that nailed the lessons of this entire chapter: **language is slippery, and assumptions are dangerous.**

On a trip to Japan, Charles wanted to sound respectful and order a simple appetizer of Nara-zuke (奈良漬け), a common pickled gourd. Zuke (漬け) is the pickling technique. In trying to be polite, he added the honorific "O-" in front of it. In Japanese, "O" can elevate a word—ōcha (tea), ōbachan (grandma). Seems harmless, right?

Except when he asked for *Onara-zuke,* he unknowingly transformed the word.

The waiter nearly collapsed from laughing. Why? Onara (おなら) means fart. With the zuke afterwards, he essentially asked for… **pickled farts.**

## Final Thought

Miscommunication can tank a deal, sink a strategy, or if you're lucky, just get you laughed at over pickled farts. Either way, the cure is the same: **learn the context, mind the culture, and never assume "yes" means "yes."**

# key lessons

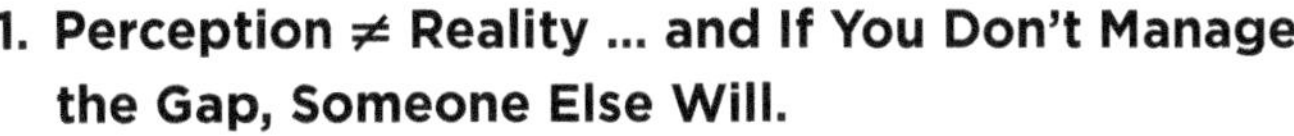

## 1. Perception ≠ Reality ... and If You Don't Manage the Gap, Someone Else Will.

Cultures build myths about themselves and each other.

Japan wasn't full of superhuman work machines, it was full of exhausted people trapped in a socially enforced performance loop.

America wasn't "lazy"—it was simply structured differently.

**The lesson:** Don't take cultural narratives at face value. Verify. Observe. Interpret. Adjust.

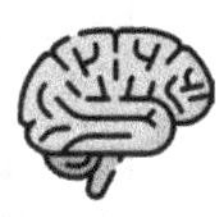

## 2. Language Is a Minefield ... Context Is King.

You can speak the words perfectly and still communicate nonsense.

Cultural dialects, outdated vocabulary, and generational language all warp meaning.

Colloquialisms like "Vanilla Windows" creates chaos. And, remember, most foreigners don't read your subtleties (colored "niceties"). Rather they translate word for word.

The lesson for professionals: **If you work with global customers, never assume translation = communication.**

Always:

- localize meaning
- verify context
- get native input
- avoid idioms

Because one wrong phrase can sink a meeting, a deal, or your dignity.

## 3. Miscommunication Isn't Cute ... It's Expensive

Whether it's a deal, a product launch, a partnership, or a global team—contextual misfires destroy outcomes.

The cure is simple but rare:

- Be curious.
- Ask questions.
- Confirm meaning.
- Never assume perception matches reality.

Do that, and you'll navigate global work far better than most.

twenty four

# Raising Five Kids … The Ultimate Management Residency

Raising five kids taught me more about management than any business book could.

When I first wrote this chapter, another title was as option: "How to lose your hair in less than 20 years."

Raising five kids is like managing a chaotic team. There's no roadmap, no clear instructions, and just a lot of learning on the fly. Sound familiar? It's the perfect training ground for leadership.

People used to say to me, "Four kids in college at the same time; how do you sleep at night?"

I would reply, "I sleep like a baby … I wake every two hours and cry."

I absolutely love my five kids. Two are my natural children from my first marriage and the other three are my former stepchildren. I say "former" because I adopted them, so they are mine. Voluntarily. Really.

## Management Boot Camp ... Raising Kids

Raising five kids taught me more about management than any business book could. The frustrations? Real. The lessons? Priceless. And, like managing a team, I eventually realized my frustration was costing me more than just patience … it was costing me my hair.

Now, I take great delight watching my kids trying to raise their own offspring and experience the process themselves. If you could only see the smile on my face.

What I didn't realize at that time, is that raising five kids was the boot camp for being a manager. As we all grew older, my patience grew too. And with it, I became a better manager.

## Patience—A Skill Earned Through Parenting

Raising kids isn't about patience as a virtue. No, it's about survival. From kids jumping off the roof into the 6-foot snowbanks to teenage tantrums, you learn to manage frustration, and that skill pays dividends in the boardroom. The same goes for managing a team—take a breath and let them figure it out. It's all part of the process.

Just like being a manager.

## Lessons from the Boss

It's hard to be a good manager when your boss isn't one. One of my earliest bosses and mentors, Roger, told me this after reading Ken Blanchard's *One Minute Manager*. Rog said, "While the book makes sense, you can't be a one-minute manager if your boss isn't one and his/her boss isn't one." The truth is you can, but it makes it a lot harder.

**The essence of leadership —empowering others.**

I was fortunate. Early in my career, I worked for a guy named Dave. He asked me to prepare some things for a meeting, and being young and brash, I said, "Sure, but isn't this your job?" Dave simply replied, "Yes, and when you can do this, you can have my job."

Dave taught me the most important leadership lesson: Empower your people. Give them the tools, trust them to do the job, and they'll rise to the occasion. That's the essence of leadership—empowering others. It's a lesson I apply every day, both in parenting and management. If I can teach my kids how to navigate the world, I can certainly help my team thrive.

Dave taught me to trust my instincts ... and to be secure enough to help others grow.

### Being a Good Manager Is like Being a Good Parent

You have to figure out the BS from what really matters. Take my son, Grant. Good kid. But he doesn't take a lot of BS either. Trust me, the apple didn't fall far from the tree.

So I get a call from my then-wife telling me Grant got in trouble in 5th grade. Apparently, his teacher was upset about something he said or did. So I called the teacher.

Teacher: Grant did something bad today.

Me: I figured. What did he do?

Teacher: He called another kid a bad name ...

Me: Okay.

Teacher: He called a kid something inappropriate.

Me: Okay (now getting a bit impatient)

Teacher: We don't like kids calling each other names using bad words ...

Me: Okay, what did he call him? (getting really impatient)

Teacher: He called a name we don't think is acceptable.

Me: Okay (now rolling eyes in my head)

Should I mention that this back and forth went for several more rounds? Finally the big moment happens … the reveal of what Grant said.

Teacher: He called <insert kid's name> a "dick"

Me: Damn it! I've told that kid a hundred times that 'dick' is an adjective, not a noun! It's a modifier like 'dick-breath', 'dick-face', or 'dick-head'. Thanks, I'll take care of it.

*click*

Cue the chaos train on the other end of the line. So much for Richard Cranium.

Being a good manager, like being a good parent, is about knowing which battles are worth fighting. This incident wasn't about a word, it was about defending my kid. The same thing I do with my team when it's appropriate that someone is overreacting.

## The Balancing Act of Being a Manager

In management, just like in life, you'll encounter bullies—people who prey on the weak or fail to respect boundaries. As a parent, you teach your kids to stand up to bullies. As a manager, you do the same for your team. It's not about playing hero; it's about creating an environment where respect is the baseline and intolerance for bad behavior is the norm.

I don't like bullies. I have a low tolerance for them, growing up post-WW2, people attacked me for being of Japanese descent.

Of course, this was before people found out about sushi. And before martial arts became popular.

I had someone that was bullying one my team members. Demanding things at once that take time to research. She told me and I called Mr. Bully's manager and had a pleasant and truthful conversation. I explained that Mr. Bully's behavior was unacceptable and his manager agreed, but explained that Mr. Bully's mother had just passed away. I suggested Mr. Bully might need some time off to deal with grief in a more productive manner.

**Managing isn't about authority ... it's about leadership.**

Mr. Bully called my team member and apologized for his behavior. Sometimes, it is helping someone understand when their actions are inappropriate. Applying a small hammer instead of a sledgehammer.

But part of being a manager is knowing when to put a stop to that. It's part of when you put on the managerial hat.

## Empathy in Leadership: Putting Yourself In Their Shoes

Managing isn't about authority … it's about leadership. Today's leaders understand their team's perspective and guide them with empathy. I've learned this from my kids, especially when it comes to their mistakes. Instead of reacting in anger or frustration, I learned to ask myself, *Why did they do this?*

A good manager sees beyond the tasks and connects with their team on a personal level. Understanding that missed deadlines might not be laziness, but a personal challenge, or that a poorly executed idea might come from a lack of experience. In my book, that's empathy at work. You work together to figure out what's needed to overcome the roadblock or obstacle.

As a parent, I learned to be empathetic. It's how you get through tantrums, teenage rebellion, and sibling rivalries. It's about seeing beyond the task at hand and understanding why someone missed the deadline or didn't execute the plan well. Empathy builds trust and trust is the foundation for effective teamwork.

### Delegation … Learning to Let Go and Yes, Keep Your Sanity

Letting go of control is another skill that parenting and management have in common. As a parent, you quickly learn that you can't do everything for your kids. You need to delegate. But more importantly, you have to trust them to handle things themselves, even when you're pretty sure they're going to screw it up. Same with management.

> Humor is a strategic tool
> in the leader's arsenal.

The more you delegate, the more the team can step forward and take ownership. Just like with my kids, I learned that giving them responsibility and allowing them to make their own mistakes is the best way to help them grow. The key? The secret sauce is to let go of control without letting go of support.

### The Importance of Humor in High-Stress Situations

Parenting is one of the most stressful jobs out there, but also the most rewarding one. Nothing like seeing your offspring launch successfully into their lives as adults. Being a parent has taught me to laugh at the ridiculousness of life and to find humor in even the most stressful situations.

Humor in high-stress situations isn't just about lightening the mood. It's about creating a space where you team can breathe and refocus. A well-timed joke or lighthearted comment can reset the atmosphere, spark creativity, and ultimately drive better results. It's a strategic tool in the leader's arsenal, just as it is in parenting.

## Grant's Hot Sauce Chaos

Back to my son, Grant. The kid has a fun spirit about him but not always the common sense factor. That's teenagers, right? It's 20 degrees out, snowing, and they're wearing short pants. At times you wonder if they're more than "a hamburger shy of a happy meal."

In high school, we got him a set of "Mike's" hot sauces as a gift, including hottest one made. Even came in its own coffin. I'm sure today's Carolina Reaper comes in a charred coffin.

One day, Grant took this coffin hot sauce to high school with him. Chaos ensued.

Some kids puked, other got their eyes burned, and paramedics were involved. Grant gets in trouble and I get a voicemail. The names have been changed to protect the guilty.

Voice message ... "Mr. Nakagawa, this is Justine Credible from the school and Grant brought hot sauce to school and it caused lots of problems including students who vomited all over the place and a student who had to go to ER for touching her eye after touching the sauce. If he every brings this to school again, we will have him charged with bringing a weapon to school."

This is *not* the voicemail you want to leave on my phone. Ever. Let's just say they quickly understood my response.

I explained they needed to understand the difference between innocent, but stupid, teenagers and the more serious discussion around weapons. I even left the definition of a weapon to help educate them.

### The Moral of the Story ... Embrace the Chaos

What's the moral of landing my kids within these pages? Management is about helping people learn from their mistakes. We all make them. In management we call these "learning moments." Even Moses made mistakes.

As parents, we didn't blame teachers for our kids' bad grades, and we didn't let them bully other kids. If they messed up, they apologized. As managers, sometimes we apologize on behalf of our team. Other times, we make them apologize themselves. But when something's BS, you call it out.

Anyone who's survived raising teens, I salute you. It's like managing chaos 24x7.

Just like being a manager.

# key lessons

### 1. Embrace the Chaos—It's Where the Real Leadership Lessons Live.

You don't become a great manager by reading books.

You become one by navigating complexity, guiding people through messes, teaching accountability, modeling empathy, and leading with steadiness through chaos.

If you can survive raising teens, along with hot-sauce ER incidents, you can survive any team dynamic.

### 2. Protect Your Team. But Correct Them When Needed.

Leaders protect publicly → Coach privately.

Your team needs to know you'll stand up for them—and also hold them accountable when they're in the wrong.

This is how a performance culture stays humane and high-quality.

### 3. Empower People Early ... It Builds Capability and Confidence.

Dave's lesson to me still stands:

Give people responsibility before they feel ready. Let them stretch, experiment, and sometimes mess up.

This is how future leaders are made: through trust, guided autonomy, and opportunities to grow.

The more you let people try, the more they rise.

twenty five

# Why You Can't Shuck and Jive

You have to know your products and your competitors' products better than the customer does—
and better than your competition.

There was a saying in the 1970s: "You can't shuck and jive." It originally referred to guitar players—basically, if you could only play three chords, you could fake it in a band. Not anymore. Today, if you only know three chords, you'll end up playing a solo gig in the unemployment line.

## You Get What You Put In

Instant answers and gratification have become the norm. If you thought competition was tough in the '80s, '90s, or even the early 2000s, buckle up. Today's competition is 1,000% fiercer.

Today's customers are smarter, more sophisticated, and they do their own research. By the time they call you, they've already made their shortlist and nearly sealed the deal. You're no longer part of the early conversation—you're playing catch-up.

Studies by 6sense, SalesLion, and RAIN Group show that between 57% and 70% of the customers' buying journey are completed before they reach out to a vendor. If you're not selected early, you're not invited to the party. The odds are you probably didn't even know it was happening. Customers have peer groups and networks; they contact each other directly for feedback before they ever bring a vendor into the room.

The astute salesperson understands this dynamic and adjusts. You have to know your products *and* your competitors' products better than the customer does—and better than your competition. If you don't, you'll be left behind.

And with GenAI's ability to manipulate and generate compelling marketing messaging that appeals directly to Kahneman's System One thinking, you're fighting an uphill battle. And it's just as dangerous as catching a javelin.

My team often gets salespeople that want help on Requests for Proposals (RFPs) and Requests for Information (RFIs). The first thing we ask them is: *"How much influence did you have in the creation of the RFP/RFI and the decision criteria?"* If the deer in the headlights look is displayed, a lot of "um," or "not much," we know from experience, the chances of winning the deal is close to zero. Not zero-zero, but close. Post-mortems on these losses are just heartbreaking.

Some companies have active GenAI programs that could completely bypass salespeople in the buying journey. Just look at some of the automated sales recommendation AI agents being developed by Amazon and Alibaba.

Bring insights that highlight your differentiators and show why you're the best solution for your customer's needs.

Sure, there are customers who only care about the lowest price. Usually, they're the most problematic ones. The true winners in sales? They're the ones who come best prepared, work in the customer's best interest, and who can read the situation to their advantage—even if that means positioning themselves for future business.

**Compete on value and build relationships that last.**

## One of the Smartest Sales Strategies I've Seen

One of the smartest salesman I know taught me how to strategically sell when it seems like you're losing on price. I've shared his lesson with many of my team members:

> When it's clear he's about to lose the deal because of price, he doesn't just accept it. He asks the customer, *"What discount did they offer you? I'd like to help you get an even better deal."* He submits a bid that forces the competition to lower their price even further.

When the low-priced deal inevitably doesn't meet expectations, who do you think the customer calls next?

Your lesson here: competitors can't keep cutting prices without eventually running themselves into the ground. It's death by a thousand cuts—or price cuts. Marginally profitable product lines don't survive the long run. Sometimes they don't survive to mid-term.

Cutting prices isn't a strategy; it's a race to the bottom. The real winners know how to differentiate strategically. And that's what this guy did. Every time. But as a realist, he knew some people only wanted the lowest price. And he had a plan for it.

Being strategic means moving beyond features or price tags. Instead, craft a compelling value proposition rooted in your customer's real pain points and business outcomes. Show how your solution uniquely solves their problem, not just how it's cheaper or flashier.

My salesman colleague was also a master storyteller. Stories sell. Share examples of how your product delivered real impact—increased revenue, reduced risk, faster time to market. This resonates more than a list of specs.

Remember: Compete on value and build relationships that last.

## You Gotta Know Your Products ... Always

I once worked for a sales manager who didn't even know what his own products did. He said, "Go sell 'Product A' to this customer." When I asked him why, his response was consistent but detached from reality. "Because you'll make quota."

Now, if I'd done what he said, I would have lost my credibility. Product A was outdated, with functionality that hadn't been relevant in over a decade. It was like trying to sell pencils and paper to someone using a PC for word processing. No one wanted them.

When I pointed out the issue with Product A's functionality, he just walked away. So, I asked him, "Do you think I could walk out of that customer's building *without* being thrown out the window if I followed your suggestion?"

This is the problem with a lot of salespeople. They don't understand their own products—or the competition. They go in blind, making suggestions they don't even believe in, and wonder why they lose credibility and fail to close the deal.

## The Instant Gratification Era

Around 2015, I … and others … noticed a shift. People started coming into the office later and leaving earlier. My company was a semi-startup. We were used to 6 a.m. starts and staying past 8 p.m. This new "come-late-leave-early" trend baffled us.

Technology was maturing—iPhones, VPNs, 4G, Slack, Google Docs—enabling remote work and "always on" availability. Coupled with a new generation of workers that prioritizing work-life balance, the expectations shifted.

**Real success demands patience, critical analysis, deeper thinking, and resilience.**

With that came the expectation of instant answers: fast, bite-sized, and consumable like popcorn at the movies. People want answers handed to them without having to understand the "why" behind them.

And that's where the problem lies.

## Managing Instant Gratification in Teams

This era of instant gratification is bleeding into our work cultures. People wants quick answers and immediate results with minimal effort … or thinking on their part.

As leaders, we must resist this impulse. Real success demands patience, critical analysis, deeper thinking, and resilience.

- Encourage your teams to slow down, ask *why*, and challenge assumptions.
- Promote curiosity, learning, and mastery over shortcuts and quick fixes. This isn't an anti-GenAI discussion—GenAI has its place—but assume answers aren't automatically correct.
- Scrutinize its responses with the same diligence you'd apply to research.

Also keep in mind: your competition is using GenAI to develop plans to take you down.

## Digging for Gold—Ask Why

Simon Sinek's TED Talk about *Start with Why* applies just as well to critical thinking. Asking *why* can uncover hidden insights.

Once, we noticed a competitor selling off parts of their portfolio —not core products, but ancillary ones. At first glance, it looked like "window dressing," a move companies use to appear attractive for acquisition.

> **Beware of the shiny-object syndrome.**

We asked, "Why are they doing this? Why now? Who might buy them?" We identified two potential buyers, and our hypothesis proved correct. The deal fell through, and shortly afterwards, the CEO left. Apparently there was a huge bonus tied to the sale.

## Developing Sharp Competitive Intelligence

In today's hyper-competitive market, competitive intelligence isn't just a nice-to-have element. Your very survival is dependent on it. You can't rely on luck or hope your products' shiny features will sell themselves.

Teams need to build their competitive insight muscles. It starts with proactively gathering intel, tracking competitor moves, and spotting market shifts early. These are things GenAI does well and much faster than a human can. But the "human in the middle" still need to review the information gathered and apply their experience to discriminate between what's real and what are false positives.

Beware of the shiny-object syndrome: AI overhype, marketing buzzwords, or superficial data that won't help you. Some of that data might be trying to misdirect you so beware. Real intelligence comes from critical thinking, context mapping, and applied experience.

Train your teams to do more than memorize specs. They must learn to interpret customer needs and competitor weaknesses. That means digging deeper: Why is that competitor winning in this segment? What pain points are they solving? Where are they vulnerable? What are their blind spots?

**The market doesn't reward fakers.**

Without that level of insight, you're not playing strategic chess … you're playing tactical checkers. And your competitors may have anticipated your moves before you make them.

## Mastery Over Shucking and Jiving: The Call to Action

Be the person your team and customers trust to have the real answers. Play the long game. Invest the time and effort needed to build trust and credibility. Show up ready, every time.

And here's the strategic truth: showing up with half-learned skills or shallow knowledge isn't risky—it's invisible. The market doesn't reward fakers. What it rewards is foresight, preparation, and the ability to act on insight before others even see the move coming.

Mastery over shucking and jiving isn't just about sales—it's about thinking ahead, anticipating shifts, and turning information into differentiated advantages. Because your next chapter isn't about what you know today … it's about seeing the patterns that will shape tomorrow.

# key lessons

## 1. To Win Today, You Must Outthink, Over-Prepare, and Outlearn Everyone.

The era of faking it is dead. The new battlefield rewards:

- critical thinking
- pattern recognition
- strategic differentiation
- depth
- early influence
- disciplined curiosity

If you rely on shallow knowledge, price cuts, or instant gratification, you're not competing—you're waiting to be replaced.

Mastery is the only moat that gives you the ability to win.

## 2. Customers Are 70% Done Buying Before You Even Show Up—So You'd Better Be Worth Their Time.

Modern buyers aren't waiting for a sales pitch. They've already researched, shortlisted, compared peer reviews, and formed opinions.

If you're not proactively shaping their thinking, you're just a late-stage checkbox. You've already lost. You just don't know it. And won't get invited to the party anyway.

**Influence early or get eliminated silently.**

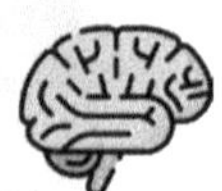

## 3. Instant Gratification Is Killing Thinking. Don't Let It Kill Your Team.

People want fast answers without understanding the why. GenAI is making everyone lazy while manipulating everyone's lives daily.

Leaders must push the opposite:

- ask deeper questions
- slow the impulse to react
- challenge surface-level assumptions
- build critical thinkers

GenAI accelerates everything—including stupidity. Your job is to enforce interpretation over shortcuts.

part five

# Passion, Legacy, and The Long Game

## Author's Note

# Passion, Legacy, and the Long Game

Have you ever wondered what all the miles, meetings, and late nights actually add up to? Whether the grind we put ourselves through really compounds into something lasting ... or just receipts from airports and goat-rodeo meetings? And what happens when you realize that time, unlike money or titles, is the one currency you can't re-earn?

That's the challenge of the long game. Most of us are trained to chase fireworks—the big win, the dramatic launch, the headline success. But castles, careers, and legacies aren't built in a day. They're built brick by brick, habit by habit, conversation by conversation. They're briskets that only get good if you cook them low and slow.

This final section is about pulling the aperture back and asking bigger questions:

- What's your ROI on sanity?
- Who carries your baton when you're gone?
- Are you compounding small wins into a fortress—or just stacking bricks in the yard?

Legacy isn't a finish-line speech. It's the ripple effect of how you invest your time, your passion, and your people. Day after day, year after year.

Here you'll find stories about careers rethought through the lens of patience and balance, about breaking free from the velvet cage of corporate life, about legacies shaped not by one big gesture but by a thousand small deposits. You'll see how leaders multiply themselves through mentoring, how families and passions create resilience, and why your unique shade of "purple"—your blend of ambition, curiosity, and relationships—is the only long game that really matters.

If the earlier parts of this book were about becoming strategic, staying strategic, and wielding intelligence as a weapon, Part Five is about playing for keeps. It's about designing a life that compounds, one that outlasts job titles and outshines resumes. Because in the end, the scoreboard isn't promotions or miles flown.

It's legacy—who carries your story forward, and how far the baton goes after you've let it go.

twenty six

# Compounding Small Wins

The slow build isn't just about the market or your team. The toughest discipline is with yourself.

Everybody loves the big, dramatic win. The last-second field goal. The knockout punch. The "we crushed Q4" headline. It's wired into us … or at least reinforced by the movies we watch.

But here's the real truth: most real wins aren't fireworks. They're bricklaying. Small, boring, almost invisible wins that stack and compound until one day: boom—you've got a castle.

*Rome wasn't built in a day*, and neither is a career, a business, or a legacy.

Musashi Miyamoto spent his entire lifetime honing his swordsmanship, only to realize half the battle was mastering his own mind. Warren Buffet didn't become the "Oracle of Omaha" overnight—his biggest compounding wins came after 50. Maya Angelou published her first autobiography at 41. J. R.R. Tolkien published his first book of *Lord of the Rings* when he was 62.

Whether on the battlefield, in investing, or in art, the lesson is the same: greatness takes time.

And here's the hard part: the slow build isn't just about the market or your team. The toughest discipline is with yourself.

## Strategic Patience for Self

Many people set ridiculous goals and deadlines. Then beat themselves up when they aren't hit. Or worse, move the goalposts mid-game because of a restless ambition that keeps circling. Add in today's instant-gratification culture, and it's a recipe for anxiety and bad decisions.

I've been there. Rushing into choices. Letting emotions call the plays. Ending up more nervous, more drained, and no happier.

Eventually, I had to stop. To sit down and really ask:

**What do I want this next chapter to look like?**
**Where am I building a fortress—and where am I just piling bricks in the yard?**

Then, someone whispers in your ear: "*The rat race is over … the rats won.*"

This isn't passive waiting. It's deliberate pacing. Playing the long game on purpose.

Careers aren't built in a day—and briskets don't cook in two hours. Whether it's stone or smoke, the principle's the same: time, restraint, and small adjustments add up to something extraordinary.

## Briskets Don't Cook in Two Hours

Barbequing—as in low and slow (not grilling)—a brisket takes time. Lots of time. Fourteen to sixteen hours if you do it right. The payoff? Slices of tender, juicy, smoke-kissed perfection. I know … barbequing is part of my DNA … I'm a master at it.

I didn't know that at first. Tried to rush it. Cranked the temp too high. Over-smoked it. The result? Shoe leather so dry even the dogs turned their noses up.

**Communication, problem-solving, leadership skills build a solid foundation for layering onto later.**

Careers are often like that. Promotions are rushed, titles chased, peers are competed against—sometimes even competing against your own manager. Too often, thoughts of speed equals progress take over. The results? What you end up serving is undercooked. Charred on the outside, raw in the middle. Tough as a boot.

The pros know better. They manage the heat. They trust the process. They don't open the lid every ten minutes. That's the difference between frustration and mastery—steady discipline, pacing, and letting small adjustments compound into something worth serving.

The truth is, brisket—like a career, or a legacy—isn't one big move. It's dozens of little ones compounding over time: trimming right, seasoning evenly, holding the fire temp steady, wrapping at the right moment, and then that critical period of resting the brisket. None of those steps are glamorous, but they turn a tough cut into something extraordinary.

A palace isn't built in a day. The brisket isn't cooked in two hours. And the long game isn't about fireworks. It's about tending the fire until the work is worth serving.

## The BBQ Playbook for Careers

Great brisket is part science, part art, and all discipline and patience. Turns out careers aren't much different. Here's the low-and-slow cookbook:

- **Season Early, Don't Overload.** Season sparingly with the right spices. Same with careers—stack the basics first. Communication, problem-solving, leadership skills build a solid foundation for layering onto later.
- **Hold the Fire Steady.** BBQ is about hours of consistency. Careers reward the same. Show up, deliver, learn, repeat. Too many people sprint hard and burn out.

- **Wrap at the Right Moment.** Pitmaster's wrap locks in the juices. In careers, that's protecting your time and energy—saying no to distractions, consolidating wins, or taking a lateral move before going up.
- **Rest Before Serving.** Slice too soon and you lose all the juices. Same with careers:  reflection, recharging, and reframing between big pushes. The pause is part of the process.

**You keep laying bricks until one day you realize the house is built.**

Briskets—and careers—don't cook in two hours. They're built low and slow, through steady effort and a rhythm you can sustain. Do it right, and when you finally serve it up, people will remember it. And they'll come back for seconds.

## The Small Steps Never Seen

With the exception of a few prodigies, the road to becoming a professional musician is a grind: daily practice, endless rehearsals, and taking every gig you can to sharpen your chops. Ask any seasoned player and they'll tell you—it takes years, sometimes decades, to "arrive."

And it's not just about hitting the right notes. Timing, intonation, dynamics, blending, articulation—it's the small but invisible refinements that turn noise into music. Musicians call it "paying your dues," and it's anything but glamorous. You keep laying bricks until one day you realize the house is built.

**Small wins don't just add up ... they multiple.**

The same holds for athletes. What looks like raw talent under the lights is almost always years of compounding, thankless reps behind the curtain.

### Steph Curry: Habit Stacking and Relentless Precision

In a 2014 *BestSelf.co* blog post, NBA performance coach Alan Stein Jr. recalled working with a young Curry. While most players were still lacing up, Curry would be on the court—taking 100-150 shots before practice officially started. And when practice ended, he refused to leave until he'd drained five free throws in a row.

That discipline wasn't about flash or show. It was habit. It was compounding. Every unseen rep was another brick in the wall, another layer of muscle memory. The effortless three-pointer you see today was built on years of invisible shots nobody clapped for.

The truth is Curry's routine works the same way as Buffet's investments do. One shot, one drill, one habit isn't much on its own. But stack them daily, and over time you've banked compound interest in skill. The market rewards capital; the game rewards preparation. Both are brutal to anyone who confuses a lucky streak with a track record.

**Lesson:** small wins don't just add up. Done with a dedicated focus, they multiply.

## Life in the Fast Lane

If compounding small wins is the quiet road to success, chasing fireworks is the fast lane to rubble. As the Eagles sang, *"Life in the Fast Lane."*

You see it in careers. Highflyers flame out because they sprint early and skip the basics. They chase the title jump, the "VP by 30," then stall when the foundation isn't there. It's the Peter Principle at work. Without the boring reps—communication, resilience, managing teams—they're brittle. One setback and they crumble.

**When the flash fades,
you have nothing to show for it.**

You see it in business. Startups raise billions, buy Super Bowl ads, and declare themselves "category killers" before they've nailed product-market fit. Momentum masquerades as substance—until it doesn't. WeWork is a case study: big boots, big hat, no cattle. Valuation fireworks, then fire sale.

And I've lived it personally. The knockout punch—betting on the big launch, the great innovation—only to realize some bricks were made of paper-mâché. The product was ready, the rest wasn't. Painful lesson: make sure the mortar cures before you build the tower.

That's the danger of the fast lane. The flash feels good in the moment. But when it fades, you're left with nothing to show for it. Small wins might feel boring, but they're what makes sure the big moments actually stick.

## Your Compounding Playbook for Life

The antidote to fireworks isn't sexy. It's stacking bricks. It's taking reps. It's compounding the small stuff until it looks inevitable.

That's the part people miss—small wins don't just add up. They multiply. A little better today makes tomorrow's effort land harder, cleaner, faster. Do that for years, and the "overnight success" isn't a miracle. It's math. Try it with your finances and you'll see it's true.

Here's what that looks like in real life:

- **Career—Brick by Brick.** Big promotions are built on invisible micro-skills: learning how to listen, write impactful emails, speaking with clarity. Each one seems trivial but stack them and suddenly people call you "leadership material."
- **Relationships—Bite by Bite.** Trust isn't forged in grand gestures. It's small, consistent acts—checking in, remembering details, showing gratitude, appreciating and noticing

your team's efforts. One bite at a time, you go from acquaintance to ally.

- **Health—Rep by Rep.** Crash diets and January sprints flame out. Twenty minutes a day—a walk, push-ups, stretching—compounds into strength and resilience. Slow is sustainable; sustainable is powerful. Beats angioplasty, trust me.
- **Strategy—Iteration Over Fireworks.** The companies who win aren't always the flashiest. They test, iterate, and refine until the flywheel turns. Amazon didn't bet it all on one product. They kept adding bricks: books, Prime, AWS. Each win looked small until it didn't. "How can I add value to everything I do?"

The compounding playbook is brutally simple: do the small, boring things long enough that they turn into big, unstoppable things.

## The Long Game of Small Wins

Here's the thing: castles, briskets, symphonies, even Steph Curry's jumper—they're all built the same way. Not by chasing fireworks, but by stacking small wins until they feel inevitable.

That's the quiet truth no one wants to hear. Big moments make headlines, but it's the boring reps that make history. The emails you sharpen, the meetings where you truly listen, the thank-yous given when no one is watching. That's the real compounding.

And here's why it matters: life isn't a sprint to the next title, the next quarter, or the next launch. It's the discipline of laying brick after brick, even when it feels invisible, even when nobody claps. Do that, and one day you'll wake up with a mansion—or a career, or a legacy—that looks inevitable to everyone else.

The takeaway? Don't get fooled by the flash. Ask yourself daily: what brick am I laying today? Build the small wins into habits. Let them stack; let them multiply. The big win you're chasing will come—not as a surprise, but as the natural result of everything you've already built.

That's the compounding effect. Quiet. Relentless. Unstoppable.

And yet, even fortresses and legacies don't stand on wins alone. The question shifts from what you build to why you build it—passion, legacy, and the long game.

It might be turning into a fractional. That's where we turn next.

# key lessons

### 1. Focus on "Directionally Correct," Not Perfect.

You don't need the perfect plan. You need the right direction and the discipline to move toward it every day.

Small progress in the right direction, not massive effort in the wrong one.

Compounding works only when the inputs are aligned with your long-term goals, not your short-term impulses.

Consistency feels boring but compounds forever.

Your future self is built from small, sustainable routines, not occasional acts of desperation.

### 2. Strategic Patience Isn't Passive. It's Choosing Purpose Over Panic.

Rushing creates burnout, bad decisions, and undercooked careers—the human equivalent of a ruined brisket.

The pros pace themselves. They hold the temperature steady. They don't open the lid every 10 minutes to see "how things are going."

Your career needs the same discipline: **Slow, steady, deliberate progress beats frenetic flailing every time.**

### 3. The World Crowns the Visible Win—But the Invisible Wins Make It Possible.

The big victories, the recognition, the promotions, the "how did they get so good?" comments: they're all by-products.

What people see is the explosion.

What they don't see is the fuse you've been quietly burning for months or years.

Build the fuse. The blast takes care of itself.

twenty seven

# To Frak or Not to Frak, That Is the Question

Legacy isn't just what you built at Company X.
It's the relationships you deepened,
the sanity you protected, and the
time you invested where it mattered most.

With apologies to William Shakespeare … some of you are wondering what the hell I'm talking about. There's a whole movement toward becoming a "Fractional" aka Frak employee … and evidence is stacking up and accumulating daily, that it is the future of work ... and maybe even today.

I was intrigued when I first heard the term "fractional work." *What did that mean?* Leaders in this space like John Arms, the host of the *WTF! —What the FRAK* podcast teaches a class on how to become a fractional "frak" executive. In fact, John is known as the "Mayor of Fraktown." I suspect it's a takeoff of Guy Fieri's "Mayor of Flavortown." Guys like John Arms and Rob Smith are intimately involved with advancement of the fractional movement.

My first exposure to fractional executives was over a lunch arranged by my friend Andreas. Two of his colleagues were introduced as fractional executives (CxO). I became intrigued by what these two fraks were saying over our delicious lunch. I'm based in Colorado and discovered that there is a local group called the Colorado Fractional Collective for Colorado-based fraks to network, socialize, and provide leads on fractional opportunities.

**To Frak isn't a fad … it's become a trend.**

In addition to John's work, noted futuristic thinkers like Rishad Tobaccoawala, author of *Rethinking Work*, notes "in 2022, more than one-third of US workers and two-thirds of those under age thirty juggled different "gigs" (rather than work full-time at one job)." Obviously, to Frak isn't a fad … it's become a trend.

## Why Should I Give a Frak?

For the older labor force, it means having the opportunity to offer your skills, experience, and insights to small and medium-sized businesses but on a part-time basis. Currently, at least, the concept of a fractional worker is a foreign concept to most large companies. But let's say for mid-sized companies, it means getting someone with years of experience and know-how for a fraction of the cost. Heck, you can't even touch a "junior" person for less than $100K nowadays (adjust this figure for whatever timeframe you are reading this). Bottom line: win-win for everyone.

And it is not just for the Gen Zers and Millennials. This applies to the Boomers and Gen Xers as well. Imagine talking to the overworked, overstressed mid-sized company executive who is trying to wear multiple hats, juggle multiple jobs, and doing a bad job at all of it. In steps the fractional executive or specialist helps take that burden off his/her shoulders and gets the job done to perfection at a fraction of the cost. It sounds almost too good to be true, but the number of fraks are growing every day. Full disclosure: I graduated from John Arms' class but have not yet taken the plunge to being a frak.

## Planes, Trains, and Automobiles

The implications of this are astounding for those of you who have spent your lives working the corporate grind. And I do mean GRIND. In at 8 a.m., out at 6, 7, 8, 9, 10 p.m. I remember when I lived in Michigan, I would work 8-6, go home to eat, bathe the kids, put them to bed and head back to the office at 8:30 p.m. and work till 11 or midnight on a regular basis. It may have been temporary insanity that drove that behavior, a potential after-effect of eating too much of the Farmington Hills' Buddy's Pizza, so delicious, or more likely—the perception that this effort would help me rise in my career faster.

In retrospect, I wish I could get those hours back.

They say with age comes wisdom and while it did help my career, in retrospect the cost was too high. Too many airplanes, hotels, shuttling from city-to-city, country-to-country, relocations, long hours, and lots of time away from the kids. My younger self thought squeezing for a half-full cup of juice was a good deal. The current iteration of myself says the juice wasn't worth the squeeze, not even close. Adding the stress that came on top, it and definitely was not the best decision of my life—or for my life. That's why I often say I have multiple degrees from the School of Hard Knocks.

## What Do You Do for the Airport?

I recall a story that my then-boss, Greg, told me. Like me, he was traveling a lot. Like a lot a lot: that's Pittsburgh-ese speak. He recalled going to one of those elementary parent-teacher meetings and the teacher asked Greg what he did for work at the airport. Perplexed, Greg said something to the equivalent of, "I don't know what the hell you're talking about." The teacher then replied that Cam, Greg's son, said he was always at the airport. Kids are funny people. They see and say things from an innocence point-of-view that is beyond endearing.

I'm sure Greg wished he had some of those hours back as well.

## Golden Handcuffs and the Velvet Cage

I share these thoughts because I believe we often don't take stock in developing a strategy for your own lives. Maybe more specifically, a *lifestyle strategy*. I may be in the minority so let me rephrase this by saying I didn't really have a strategy for my life, career, and family … or my sanity.

Referring back to Arthur Brooks' book *From Strength to Strength,* I can now see why—during the later parts of my career —I became increasingly frustrated. It is part of what can be thought of as a "Golden Handcuffs-Velvet Cage" type of syndrome. It is why you stay in a corporate job too long—longer than you should—and end up frustrated with "the system." It is easy to get used to the comfort of the known, even if you hate it, perks that are becoming fewer by the year, fear of the unknown, and even changing your self-identity. I often hear from others that being stuck in middle management with a lack of career advancement is now corporate slang for "The No-Man's Land of Ambition" … you know ... too senior to be ignored and not senior enough to make real change.

You may have been led to believe—either intentionally or not—that much of your self-identity is tied up in your *job*. There is some intrinsic value you get that is associated with your job and career. I remember speaking with the CEO of one of the companies where I was employed and he marveled at the answers he received when he asked an employee, "What do you do?" and the employee would wax poetic about the job, how much he/she loves their job, putting in countless hours, sacrificing time with the family, etc. The CEO told me, "That's really sad … the only identity is with the job. What an awful life."

## The ROI of Sanity

This begs the question, "How can we get a better ROI on our sanity?" I've been more fortunate than some. I've had outside interests that I am passionate about—my family, my music projects and bands, competitive BBQing, and now my grandkids, and public speaking.

**Get your frak on.**

I realized I've a better ROI on Sanity than many others. And for that, I am grateful to my wife, family, and friends who have made the journey enjoyable.

That means measuring your ROI has to go beyond your career and compensation.

- Do you have peace of mind?
- What is your presence with your family … is it just superficial?
- Are you doing things that make you and your family happy?
- Do you suffer from constantly being tired and feeling burnt out?
- What is your ROI of sanity?

Tying back to the concept of the frak worker … skip the corporate HR gauntlet and go straight to work. Real work with meaningful results. Shed the absurdity of the corporate job hunt, traditional resumes, endless interviews and the ghosting that follows. I love the idea of working with a couple of clients, having time for my kids and grandkids, traveling for fun, spending more time with my wife, and cultivating new areas of interest. And—I think—frak is the answer to getting that better ROI on sanity too.

So get your frak on!

### Breaking the Frame

Here's the truth: most of you were handed a script. *Go to school. Land a job. Climb the ladder. Retire with a gold watch and a pension.* But the script doesn't fit anymore and hasn't for 30 years. Hell, pensions barely exist. And the gold watch? That's just a Fitbit with your steps tracked by HR.

> Fractional work gives you a way to keep creating ....

What fractional work really does is break that frame. It's not about working less—it's about working differently. It's reclaiming your time and sanity while still putting your skills to work in ways that matter. For some, it's about flexibility. For others, it's about impact. For me, it's about not looking back at 80 and realizing I traded my best years for PowerPoint slides and airport lounges.

### The Pivot from Identity to Legacy

If the velvet cage of corporate life tricks you into thinking your worth is your title, fractional work is the jailbreak. It forces you to ask: *Who am I when I'm not my job?* That's a terrifying but liberating question. Because once you start answering it, you stop clinging to identity and start thinking about legacy.

Legacy isn't just what you built at Company X. It's the relationships you deepened, the sanity you protected, and the time you invested where it mattered most. Fractional work gives you a way to keep creating value while also living a life that feels like yours.

## The Takeaway: Sanity Has ROI

At the end of the day, the metric isn't billable hours or titles climbed. The real measure is whether you traded your time for something meaningful. ROI of sanity beats ROI of salary.

So whether you jump into fractional work or not, the question is worth asking: *What would it look like to stop chasing the script and start building my own?*

Because the real win isn't becoming a frak. It's realizing you get to decide how to spend your time, your skills, and your life.

And that decision, unlike the corporate ladder, is entirely yours.

That shift forces a harder question: who are you without your job title? Boomers and Gen Xers were raised to see work as identity. Millennials and Gen Zers know better: resilience comes from variety. Life, like markets, demands a portfolio. Your core, your growth, and your priceless assets all have to balance—or you risk going bankrupt where it matters most.

# key lessons

### 1. Fractional Work = Freedom Without the Midlife Identity Crisis.

Becoming a "frak" isn't some Gen Z side-hustle-fever dream—it's a real path for Boomers, Gen X, and Millennials who are done sacrificing sanity for corporate drama.

Fractional work lets you use your hard-earned expertise without the endless meetings, political landmines, and HR obstacle courses that feel like a cross between *American Ninja Warrior* and *The Hunger Games.*

It's impact without indentured servitude.

### 2. Champagne Results on a Beer Budget—Fractional Execs Are the Perfect Answer.

Mid-sized businesses need deep expertise but can't afford a full-time CxO.

Enter the fractional executive:

- senior impact
- part-time cost
- zero nonsense
- everyone wins

Especially you—because you can finally stop pretending "the grind" is noble and start delivering value without sacrificing your soul.

### 3. Golden Handcuffs Feel Nice ... Right Up Until the Circulation Stops.

Comfort + fear + identity = the Velvet Cage.

You stay because it's familiar, even if the familiarity burns.

Fractional work forces a bigger, braver question:

**Who are you when your job title isn't your personality?**

The answer is usually healthier, happier, and significantly less exhausted.

twenty eight

# The Great Divide

Legacy is about who still tells your stories when you're gone.

One of my bosses and mentors, Dave, gave me some great advice when I was young: when you're gone and buried, nobody is going to say he was a great worker and put in a lot of hours. The only people that matter are your family and kids—they'll carry on your legacy and memories of you.

Many of the Boomers (I'm one of them) and Gen Xers were raised believing work was our identity. Gen Zers see it differently—and better. Some know work is just one stream of income. Diversify—and when one dries up, you're not sunk. Side projects, passion pursuits, and alternate income gives you them resilience that my generation often lacked.

As I've gotten older, I've realized my career is a part—an important one, yes—but only a part of my life. With grandkids in the picture, I'm rethinking this next stage and coming up with a radically different picture for my future.

I've come to see life the same way I see markets: as a portfolio.

- **Core assets:** your career.
- **Growth assets:** side projects, skills, hobbies that expand you and create happiness.
- **Priceless assets:** family, health, legacy—the things that really matter.

That's the competitive intelligence lens turned inward. If you wouldn't run your company with a single revenue stream, why run your life that way?

## What's Your Legacy?

When I interviewed to lead a competitive team, the hiring VP asked me: *"What's your legacy going to be?"* Easy answer: family, music, and career—in that order. Others struggled to answer the question.

I'm very fortunate: a wonderful wife as my partner and cornerstone of our family, five kids, and five grandkids, so far. All five of our kids call me "Dad"—a title I wear proudly and humbly. We built strong foundations as a family, and now I get to watch them build their own. I officiated at our youngest son's wedding and baptized our grandson. Those are dividends that *matter.*

Legacy is about who still tells your stories when you're gone.

## Variety as Resilience

Legacy also comes from the passions that round out a life. For me, that's music, BBQing, scouting, and giving back to professional communities.

Music's been a common thread since sixth grade—nearly 50 years on trumpet and now arranging charts and producing music for a UK label. That passion hasn't faded, just evolved.

Barbecue started as competition, now I judge with the Kansas City Barbecue Society (KCBS). My wife and I cofounded a scouting troop 25+ years ago that's still thriving. And I've poured back into the Strategic and Competitive Intelligence Professionals (SCIP) Association, Product Development and Management Association (PDMA), and now as Co-Executive Director of the Society for Artificial Intelligence in CI (SAICI, pronounced "psy-kee") to help shape the next generation of product managers, marketers, strategists, and competitive intelligence professionals.

**Variety isn't distraction —it's resilience.**

Thread them together and the picture is clear: variety isn't distraction. It's resilience. Every one of those "side dishes" made me a better leader, a better father, and a better human.

My wife teases me, *"You're a busy boy."* She's right. But busy with purpose beats busy with grind every time. And, I have lots more planned for the future.

## The Competitive Intel Turned Inward

You spend your career analyzing markets, rivals, and blind spots. But consider this: most of you never run that same analysis on yourselves.

Think about it.

- **SWOT for Self.** Strengths are easy. Weaknesses you rationalize. Opportunities you ignore if you're too focused on work. Threats—burnout, family strain, health scares—you wave off until it's too late.
- **Blind Spots.** You pride yourself on spotting weak signals in markets yet miss the obvious ones in your own life: missed birthdays, anniversaries, rising stress, eroding relationships.

- **Pattern Recognition.** You can map a rival's roadmap but can't always read the signals in your own life that say, *slow down.*

The truth is competitive intelligence without self-intelligence is half-baked. If you can't recognize patterns in your own life, what good are they in the market?

Applying CI to self, forces the hard but necessary questions:

- Am I investing in the *right* places?
- Where am I overexposed?
- What blind spots am I ignoring because they're uncomfortable to confront?

It's humbling. But it's also freeing. When you treat your life with the same rigor you treat a market analysis, you realize the only scoreboard that matters isn't career and titles—it's legacy, sanity, and the people who'll remember you.

## Passion with a Purpose

Passions aren't just hobbies. They can be all consuming.

Take my Chase project. Chase was a powerhouse '70s horn band whose leader and several members died in a plane crash. Their written charts were lost, so I set out to recreate two of them. Two grew to fifty. Over eight years, and with encouragement and review/contributions from the surviving members, I rebuilt their library note-for-note. My charts were used by the surviving members to perform their "Chase Revisited" concerts 2010-2014.

Insane? Maybe. Obsessive? Definitely. But it mattered. It gave fans a way to hear the music as it was but silenced during its apex. And it reminded me: passion projects teach you the same lesson as combining small wins. One chart, one bar, one note at a time until the goal is met.

## Micro-Investments That Compound

We think about legacy in big gestures: all-inclusive family vacations to a Hawaii, milestone celebrations, the big family trip. But the truth? It's the small deposits that accumulate and grow over time.

The random call to your kids just to ask, *"How are things going?"* A couple of hours on Saturday at the driving range just to hang out and catch up. Sharing small talk with your grandchild, while your adult kid listens in from the next room, smiling at the closeness between you.

**Balance isn't soft. It's strategy.**

It's sitting in the bleachers at those gymnastic practices, cheer competitions, sports games, and high school plays. It's about being *there and present.*

At the time, these actions feel small. In hindsight, they're everything. Each one silently telegraphs: *I care; I'm here.*

The big family events are nice—skiing, vacationing, theme parks. But it's the small things that lay the foundation for building a family.

Do them consistently and your family relationship portfolio grows—imperceptible day-by-day, until it's transformed into a fortune of memories, or as my kids call it "core memories growing up."

## Balance Is the Operative Word

No financial advisor worth his/her weight would tell you to dump everything into one stock, one property, or a pile of gold bars under your bed. Why? Because when that one market tanks, so do you. The smart play is diversification—spread the risk, smooth the ride, and give yourself a buffer against the inevitable ups and downs.

Work-life balance is the same playbook. If you're "all-in" on career and nothing else, you're exposed. A bad quarter, a toxic boss, or a round of layoffs doesn't just dent your job—it guts your identity. The cost? Burnout, broken health, strained relationships, and the kind of regrets you can't expense away.

Balance isn't soft. It's strategy. Diversify your life. Invest in your career but expand through hobbies, side projects, and deepen relationships that last.

### Don't Ignore the Risk Dashboard

Here's the scary part: most people see the warning lights but ignore them anyway. They put the pedal to the metal on the highway of burnout and blow through every flashing sign.

The signals are obvious—irritability, skipped workouts, never seeing your kids, waking up at 3 a.m. stressed—and waved off like they were simply background noise.

If this were your business, you'd never ignore those signals of impending collapse. Yet when it's your health, your family, and your sanity—you rationalize, postpone, make excuses and tell yourselves, *"just one more quarter."*

By the time the light turns red, it's often too late.

## Keeping It Fresh

For me, the antidote to burnout has been keeping fresh interests outside of work. I keep a running list and re-prioritize it each year: things I want to learn, books to read, hobbies to try, health goals, family commitments. Each year, I pick three to five to make real.

It could be getting to every grandchild's birthday party, exploring a new skill, or spending focused time with one of our kids. The point is simple: without goals that excite you, you risk fading into the sunset. And I don't plan on fading quietly.

Balance isn't the absence of ambition. It's opening the aperture wide enough to see more than the next deadline. It's family, friendships, curiosity, passions—the things that keep you young at heart. I wake each day looking forward to what's next.

## The Wide Lens Close Up

Work narrows your focus. Quarter-by-quarter, meeting-by-meeting, title-by-title—the aperture tightens until all you see is the next deadline, the next deal, the next rung on the ladder. For years, I mistook that for clarity. In truth, it was tunnel vision.

Clarity doesn't come from zooming in tighter. It comes from pulling back, opening the frame, and taking in the whole picture. It's when you see the grandkids blowing out the candles. Thanking the spouse who's been your anchor through every storm. The friends who've walked beside you when the job didn't. The passions that make you feel alive when the calendar is stripped of titles and roles.

**It's your balance sheet of meaning.**

This is the wide lens of legacy. And like any great lens, it forces you to prioritize. The background noise fades. The subjects that matter come into sharp relief.

The lesson is simple but not easy: balance isn't something you stumble into. It's something you design. It's portfolio thinking applied to life—intentionally allocating time and energy into assets that will matter long after the office lights go out.

So here's the question to leave with—if someone were to look through the wide lens of your life today, what would be in focus? Would it only be the office? Or would they see people, passions, and purposes that will carry your story when you're no longer in the room?

The answer isn't just your legacy. It's your balance sheet of meaning. And it's yours to shape—starting now.

And when it comes to leadership, the same lesson applies. We don't need more corporate "heroes" pulling all-nighters for applause. What teams need are leaders who build capacity, who multiply themselves, who leave something that lasts long after they're gone. The long game of leadership is legacy, not headlines.

# key lessons

### 1. A Career Is a Slice of Life, Not the Whole Pie.

Boomers and Gen Xers were raised to believe work was identity.

Millennials and Gen Zers figured out the truth earlier: **Your job is just one income stream—not your purpose, not your legacy, not your self-worth.**

Thinking of life as a portfolio—career, passions, relationships—creates resilience no job ever will.

### 2. You Wouldn't Run a Company on One Revenue Stream, Why Run Your Life That Way?

A diversified life isn't indulgent—it's intelligent.

- Core assets (career) matter.
- Growth assets (skills, hobbies, side projects) expand you.
- Priceless assets (family, health, legacy) outlive you.
- Ignoring any one of these creates personal "market risk."

**Balance is not soft—it's strategy.**

### 3. It's About the Stories When You're Gone

Leadership isn't the grind.

Legacy isn't your résumé.

The scoreboard that matters is family, sanity, purpose, curiosity, and the lives you shaped along the way.

Design your portfolio intentionally—or someone else will do it for you.

twenty nine

# We Don't Need Another Hero

A leader builds capacity so the team can solve tomorrow's problems.

Borrowing from Tina Turner's classic lyrics revealed in "We Don't Need Another Hero" and celebrated in the movie, *Mad Max Beyond Thunderdome,* I can't help but think about leadership. The workplace doesn't need more heroes swooping in to save the day. We've got plenty—PLENTY—of managers chasing headlines and firefighting. What we really need are leaders who leave something lasting behind.

A hero solves today's problem. A leader builds capacity so the team can solve tomorrow's problems. Heroes want the spotlight that screams LOOK AT ME! Leaders want to hand it off. Heroes burn out; leaders scale out.

The long game isn't about being remembered as the hero. It's about being remembered by the people you elevated—the ones who grew stronger because you invested in them. That's legacy.

I've seen teams addicted to the corporate "hero." You know them—the one that pulls the all-nighter, rescues the broken deal, or hacks together the impossible fix in a pinch. It's impressive but brittle. Pull that person out and the system collapses. That's not resilience … that's dependence.

The real legacy work is creating systems, culture, and successors who thrive without you. In the end, your career won't be measured by how many fires you put out but by how many people you set on fire with passion, clarity, and confidence.

So, no. We don't need another hero. Leaders are needed who are willing to play the long game.

## Not Easy, but it Doesn't Need to Be Hard

A leader has to make tough calls at times, balancing competing priorities, and sometimes absorbing blame while giving away credit. That's never "easy." It requires courage, humility, and consistency. And all of this can wear on you.

**Embrace the servant mindset.**

Where it gets harder than it has to be is when leaders complicate it for themselves. Chasing perfection, micromanaging, trying to be the hero, or confusing activity for productivity. Add ego to the mix, and you've got a recipe for disaster, ineffectiveness, and losing the respect of your team.

The basics never go out of style: listening, clarity, consistency, and investing in your people.

## Metamorphosis: from Manager to Leader

Fortunately, there are managers who want to make the shift. It takes commitment and, often, a fundamental mindset change. Emotional Intelligence (EQ) helps. So does reframing how you see your role.

Go from executing the plan to painting the picture of why the plan matters. This means learning to tell the story of where you're going, not what needs to be done.

Embrace the servant mindset: instead of "my team reports to me," it becomes, "I report to my team." Impact is measured by how much stronger, capable, and confident your people become.

Leaders live with constant ambiguity and conflict. The key is figuring out *what ropes to skip, and which ones to jump* or as singer Kenny Rogers reminded toe-tapping listeners: *know when to hold them and when to walk away*. Managers seek order and predictability.

## From Arsonist to Firefighter

In Chapter 10, *The Discipline of Execution*, I told the story of someone who was both arsonist and firefighter—creating problems just so they could play the hero. That's toxic.

But sometimes, leaders do have to play both roles with a very different objective. As I used to tell my team, *"Sometimes you have to light the trash can on fire."* Not to make yourself look good, but to force attention on a problem being ignored.

**All my charts and arguments hadn't worked.**

Big companies are full of noise. Priorities compete, distractions multiply, and important issues get buried. A well-timed "trash can fire" cuts through the static. The difference is motivation: one is self-serving, the other serves the team.

One time, I had to light the trash can myself. I was struggling to convince my development team on a critical set of features. Every attempt landed on deaf ears. *"We don't see the need,"* was routinely tossed back at me, even when I threw data at them. Customers grew impatient. Nothing changed.

So I set up a meeting … a "Summit." Publicly, that's what I called it. Privately, I knew it was time to light the fire.

The customers were household names. Development reluctantly showed up, ready to defend its position: *"We can already do this today."* The customers cut them off with: *"That's not how we operate. That's not how our environments run."*

In that moment, I watch the light bulbs go on—and the fire catch. Developers weren't just hearing requirements; they were hearing *why* it mattered from the source. By the end of the meeting, they were making commitments, sketching timelines, and reenergized around the product. The customers walked out recommitted too.

All my charts and arguments hadn't worked. But one well-timed fire did.

The secret: light the trash deliberately, selectively, and infrequently. Too often, and it's just noise. Done right, it's leadership.

## Succession as the Real Long Game

At one job I had over twenty direct reports. A small village had been created. My weeks were a blur of 1:1s, with catch-up bleeding into nights and weekends. Then life threw me a curveball: a medical event that landed me in ICU for ten days and four months of recovery.

**If you're not building a legacy … you're just running a shift.**

While I was out, my boss tried to cover for me. That's when reality hit: we had no succession plan. What looked like a smooth-running machine was being held together by invisible work.

Here's the irony: I'd always prided myself on the "make it look easy" approach. To my bosses, it looked like I could do the job blindfolded while juggling plates and reading at the same time.

That trick helped me get promoted, but it also hid the sheer load I was carrying.

My absence shocked my boss. Shocked at how much work there was, amazed at how I made it look effortless. When I came back, we set up a plan to mentor someone to take my place. It was a smart and essential move that we should've made long before.

It took me two years to build up my successor. Not a mini-me, but someone with the same values and care for the team plus his own style. When the day comes, I would trust him completely without any reservations.

Here's the thing: senior execs always do this. They're constantly grooming successors. But most managers? They don't. And that's the flaw. If you're not preparing the next leader, you're not building a legacy … you're just running a shift. Is that what you want?

## The Invisibility of Good Leadership

Here's the curse of being good at your job: the better you are, the less anyone notices. Really.

Great leadership often looks boring from the outside. No drama. No flames shooting from the sales organization. No "hail Mary" rescues. Just good ole steady-Eddie running smoothly. Ironically, that invisibility can be dangerous—because when you make it look easy, people assume it *is* easy.

*Capisci?*

I've learned this the hard way. When I came back from medical leave, my boss admitted something: *"I had no idea how much you were doing."* That's not unusual. Most leaders don't.

Real leadership isn't visible in PowerPoints or status reports. It lives in the quiet work of clearing roadblocks, giving credit, absorbing blame, coaching through uncertainty, and anticipating problems before they can turn into two-alarm dumpster fires. It's *getting the shit done.* The firefighter gets the award because the fire is visible. The leader who prevents the fire rarely gets recognized at all. Not even honorable mention. That's the paradox. And the frustration.

## A Challenge for Leaders and Wannabes

If you want to test whether you're building legacy or just running on hero fuel, ask yourself:

- If I vanished tomorrow, what would fall apart?
- Who am I mentoring right now who could step in?
- What invisible work am I doing that no one else sees … and how can I make it teachable?

**If you want to be a leader, stop chasing the cape.**

If the answers make you uncomfortable, that's the point. Good leadership should outlast you. Heroes want to be remembered for saving the day. Leaders should be remembered for building people who can save tomorrow.

## Whatcha Gonna Do?

If you want to be a leader, stop chasing the cape. Heroes are exciting but fragile. When they're gone, so is the magic.

Leaders are multipliers. The long game isn't about how many times you ended up in the spotlight. It's about how many times you shined it on others. It's not about the fires you fought, but the sparks of passion, clarity, and confidence you ignite in people around you.

Fires will always come. The question is: will your team know how to handle them without you?

Here's my call to you:

- Stop trying to be the hero.
- Start building leaders.
- Play the long game.

That's the real measure of leadership. Not being the arsonist, not being the firefighter, but being the builder of systems, culture, and successors who thrive long after you've left the scene.

Which brings me to the real point: legacy isn't a solo act. It never is. It's not the plaque on the wall or the gold watch at retirement. Rather, it's a relay race. The baton you hand to your kids, your mentees, your colleagues. The ripple effects you'll never see but echo on because you invested in people who carry your fingerprints into places you'll never go.

# key lessons

### 1. Hero Culture Feels Impressive - But It's Actually Organizational Fragility.

Corporate heroes look shiny: late nights, big saves, rescue missions.

But if one person's absence collapses the system? That's not strength—**it's structural failure disguised as brilliance.**

If everything falls apart when you vanish? You weren't leading: you were hoarding responsibility.

Succession isn't optional.

It's the proof you built something that outlasts you.

Real leaders remove single points of failure instead of becoming one.

### 2. The Manager → Leader Shift Is a Metamorphosis, Not a Promotion.

Managers execute plans. Leaders articulate the *why.*

Managers seek order. Leaders navigate ambiguity.

Managers want compliance. Leaders build capability.

This isn't skill substitution—it's identity transformation.

### 3. Start Building the Heroes

The long game isn't about how brightly you burned.

It's about who you ignited.

It's about the systems, culture, and successors who thrive even when you've left the building.

**Leadership is about multiplication—not martyrdom.**

thirty

# Legacy Is a Team Sport

Legacy isn't an addition equation,
it's multiplication.

Too many people categorize legacy as a "lifetime achievement award"—something that is hoisted at the finish line. Wrong—this isn't a Hallmark channel movie. Legacy isn't a plaque on the wall or a line in your résumé. It's more like a relay race. It comes when you hand off the baton and the people you've mentored, raised, and invested in carry it forward.

Our scout troop is still thriving 25 years later, long after I handed off the leadership reins. Team members I mentored are running competitive intelligence, product management, and strategy teams of their own. I'm betting my grandkids will tell stories I'll never hear. Legacy isn't a solo album; it's the music they sing because they were part of the band.

Legacy isn't about a point-in-time event. It's every person you touched along the way. It's the shared memories, the time invested, the fingerprints you leave on people who keep playing the song. Guess what? If you're reading this book, you've still got time to start or add to your legacy.

## You're Never Alone

Nobody makes a legacy on their own. Even people like Steve Jobs didn't fly solo. There were lots of people on his journey that provided that "must support" along the way. Not only people like Woz, but others like Mike Markkula, Jef Raskin, and Tony Fadell. They helped cement Steve's legacy.

Would you remember Steve if the Mac flopped? iPhone was a failure? Nobody bought the iPod? No, you remember him as an innovator and visionary because he surrounded himself with people who helped bring his dreams to life successfully.

**No legacy is ever solo.**

Walt Disney had his brother Roy and Ub Iwerks to help him bring Mickey Mouse to life. Though Walt is often credited with Mickey, Ub actually created the character in a matter of weeks culminating in Steamboat Willie.

Oprah Winfrey had Gayle King and a team of producers who carefully shaped her show and enabled her to build Harpo Productions into the multimedia giant it is today.

The credits at the end of a *Star Wars* movie lists thousands of people involved with the filming, casting, editing, and final production … even though it was the brainchild of George Lucas.

No legacy—business, cultural, or personal—is ever truly "solo."

## Mentorship Multiplication

The best part of mentoring people is watching them launch into the next phase of their career and skyrocketing into becoming superstars. As managers, a surge of pride is felt … but that's only half the story. Have you ever considered how those launches multiply back into *your* career and legacy?

Every person you mentor carries a piece of you with them. When they succeed, your fingerprints are on their success. When they teach others, they echo the lessons you once shared. That ripple effect turns into waves you may never see, but it's still a factor in your tide rising.

And it's not just one-directional. Mentees sharpen you. Their energy, ideas, and challenges stretch you, make you better than you were before. Mentorship isn't a gift you hand down—it's an exchange that compounds for both of you.

And when you launch multiple superstars, you gain a reputation for identifying and nurturing talent. Do it once and it might be a coincidence. Do it multiple times and people want to become part of your team.

Legacy isn't an addition equation, it's multiplication. The people you lift don't just carry your work forward—they multiply it in ways that outlast you. That's how a career becomes a legacy.

## Being in the Middle

Even if you're a middle manager, you're multiplying impact everyday: up, down, and sideways. We all know the jerk at work who won't lift a finger to help, never has time, and hijacks every meeting.

The real difference-maker is the leader-in-the-middle who plays for the "we." They contribute, they connect, and they even make difficult people better just by showing up. Their influence spreads in every direction.

One tactic I've always used is my "*no surprises*" policy. My job, as I tell every boss I've ever had, is "to make you look good." That's not brown nosing … that's being smart. That means giving a heads-up when something might blow up, before it hits. Not Chicken Little panic at every shadow, but selective, credible warnings when there's a real chance of trouble.

Being in the middle isn't a weak spot. It's a leverage point. If you do it right, you're not just managing in all directions, you're multiplying.

## Being OG and the Ripple Effect

At a recent conference I was walking the floor, catching up with old friends and meeting new faces, when someone in her early 30s lit up and said, "Oh, I know who you are! You're the OG (slang: Original Gangsta) of strategy and competitive intelligence. We've all heard of you and I'd love 30 minutes if you've got it."

OG? The OG! Really!?? I almost looked over my shoulder to see who she was talking to. It was funny, humbling, and surreal. Then it hit me: I've been helping younger practitioners for years—sharing advice, listening to their struggles, nudging them towards better outcomes. I wasn't keeping score. I was just giving.

**Legacies are invisible ripples moving outwards.**

And yet here I was, meeting someone for the first time who already knew me by reputation. That's when I realized: the ripple effect was at work.

Legacy doesn't stop when you leave the room. It often grows in ways you'll never see. A scout I mentored is a leader in his business community and leads campouts today, teaching kids who were born long after I hung up my uniform. A mentee I hired early in her career now runs her own team, and she tells me she's teaching the lessons I once taught her. Lessons that go beyond the profession. Lessons about life.

That's how legacies work: invisible ripples moving outwards, multiplying year after year. People you'll never meet inherit your lessons secondhand. They may or may not know your name, but they'll feel your fingerprints. That's the power of compound influence—it travels farther than you ever imagine.

## Building Your Brand Daily

Too many people think "legacy" is reserved for end-of-career retirement speeches. It's not. Legacy is built in every hallway conversation, every late-night email, every time you choose to show up with integrity. The "jerk at work" leaves a legacy too, just not one anybody wants to carry forward.

Every interaction is a deposit in your legacy account. Sometimes it's big: mentoring someone into a promotion that feels great to support. Sometimes it's small: like being the steady, calm voice in a tense meeting asking the questions that takes the emotion out of the room. Either way, those deposits stack up. And they don't need FDIC protection—they're safeguarded by those you touched.

Legacy isn't something you tack on at the end; it's what you've been building all along. Quietly. Daily. Moment by moment. And one day, those deposits will be the compound interest that multiplies far beyond you.

## Passing the Baton Revisited

Back to where we started: legacy is a relay race. The best measure of your impact isn't the applause at the finish line—it's how well the next runners carry the baton. Did you equip them? Encourage them? Set them up for success?

**Everyone leaves a legacy.**

And don't forget … you've got more than one baton. The handoff to your kids looks different from the one to your mentees. They're running races of their own. If the time you spent with them was meaningful, that baton should give them momentum—helping them skip the blisters, avoid tripping over their shoelaces, and find the right sized shoes for their stride.

The real beauty? Each person you hand the baton to will one day hand it off again. Legacy isn't just about your race—it's about the chain of events and runners you set in motion. Your voice, your lessons, and your fingerprints are carried with them after you've left the track.

Your legacy isn't measured by your split time. It's measured by how far the baton goes after you've let it go.

## Legacies Aren't a Choice

Everyone leaves a legacy. You don't get a choice in the matter anymore than you get a choice about taxes. The questions are will it be good or bad? Will it be deliberately intentional? Or will you be satisfied with some random outcome? You can drift through your career, leaving behind scraps of frustration and unfinished work, or you can choose to build a legacy worth handing off.

The multiplication effect is already at work. You're touching people whether you intend to or not. The challenge is deciding *what you want to multiply.* Cynicism? Fear? Or courage, generosity, and vision?

At the end of the day, legacy isn't about you. It's about what keeps moving because of you.

# key lessons

### 1. Nobody Builds Anything Great Alone—Your Legacy Is a Team Effort.

Behind every visionary is an army of contributors who helped breathe life into the dream.

Jobs had Woz and Markkula.

Walt had Roy and Ub Iwerks.

Oprah had Gayle and a world-class production team.

You have your people too ... mentors, partners, colleagues, family. **Your greatness is multiplied through them.**

### 2. Your Ripple Effect Travels Farther Than You'll Ever Know.

The scout you trained teaches kids today you'll never meet.

The mentee you coached now shapes her own teams.

People know you by reputation before they meet you ... because your influence outran your presence.

That's the magic of legacy: **your impact keeps moving long after you've left the room.**

### 3. Legacy: It's About Who Goes Further Because You Showed Up.

The measure of a life isn't applause, titles, or trophies. It's momentum.

It's the people running farther, faster, and stronger because you invested in them.

**Legacy is not what you leave.**

**Legacy is what you launched.**

thirty one

# The ROI of Time ... The Currency You Can't Re-earn

Time isn't infinite, and it sure as hell isn't interchangeable.

Money comes and goes. Titles change. Even reputations can be rebuilt. But time? Once it's gone, it's gone. There are no refunds, no exchanges, no rainchecks. Yet most spend time like it's Monopoly money: burning hours in pointless meetings, chasing inbox zero, or sprinting through airports thinking you're winning. Spoiler alert: you're not.

I've got over 1.5 million miles on a major airline and a shiny "metal-for-life" status with a big hotel chain. Let me be blunt: those aren't achievements. Instead, they're tombstones for time. A sad testimony of how much of my life I traded away pursuing the golden ring at the corporate circus. Chasing windmills, eating too many midnight hotel burgers, running on too little sleep before the next round of "urgent" activity. And sitting through enough goat-rodeo meetings to last three lifetimes.

At some point, you wake up and realize: not my circus, not my monkeys. And honestly, even Monopoly jail looks better than another goat-rodeo meeting. You don't even want a Get Out of Jail Free card.

Another philosophical question for your musing is: "If I only have five more years to live, what would I do with my time?"

### Urgent Screams, Important Whispers

Have you ever noticed how people chase the loudest voice in the room? During the latter part of my career, I would sit in a meeting wondering why these "tiger teams" were chasing the loudest voice instead of the quiet one that mattered. The quiet ones often had identified the real issue needing to be addressed. Loud isn't always right and quiet isn't always wrong.

The problem: corporate life trains you to follow urgency. Those "must attend" fire-drill meetings called at the last minute with the list of misidentified priorities. Status update meeting that gobbles two hours at a time like Godzilla consuming buildings. Looking at endless PowerPoints—as a businessman and politician pointed out years ago—most PowerPoints don't have much power and don't make a point.

How many hours of your life did you trade for noise that was meaningless, and nobody remembers much about … except it was a waste of lots of people's time. How many have you wasted?

Meanwhile, the important stuff never shouts: a grandkid's birthday, a late-night band rehearsal, a Saturday BBQ competition judging event. Those don't flash red on the calendar, but they pay dividends that compound for decades. My grandkids will remember me being there when they blew out the candles.

I've learned that urgency is like Chinese food: tastes good in the moment but leaves me hungry in the next hour. By contrast, important tastes like the slow-cooked brisket: quiet, steady, nourishing. Sticks with you.

## I Can Do a Million Things at Once

I can do a million things at once. Can't you? Of course not. Nobody can. But bosses love pretending you can by piling more on your plate. They call it "delegation." I call it "death by bricklaying." One brick at a time until you collapse.

**Every yes is an invisible no.**

I created a survival trick: always say "yes"—but with a twist. When the boss says, "I need you to take this on," my answer became, "Sure, happy to. Which one of these other priorities should I drop to make room?"

That move changes the game. You're not saying no—you're forcing your boss to pick what actually matters. It saves you from the blame game later when something inevitably slips.

Time ROI lesson? You don't get extra plates. Protect the one you've got, and make the boss own the menu.

## The Hidden Cost of Free Time

Opportunity cost. That's the price tag attached to every so-called "free" request. One extra call, one quick meeting, one volunteer task. None of it is free. Every yes is an invisible no—to your family, your health, or your sanity.

I've learned this the hard way. When you manage over twenty people, you don't have "leftover" time. So I got more selfish with it. If someone on my team was already in a meeting, he/she could debrief me instead me sitting through it. Do I really need to watch another product demo? Or sit in an all-hands that's more rah-rah than substance? Answer: NO.

Some people call time "fungible." Time isn't infinite, and it sure as hell isn't interchangeable. Every "free" yes steals from something that matters.

Here's a thought experiment: imagine every request on your calendar had a $1,000 bill stapled to it you had to pay. Would you still say yes so freely? Probably not. Because this isn't Monopoly. You don't get to pass GO and collect more hours.

### Time for Being Kind to Strangers

Not every ROI calculation is cold math. Sometimes the best return comes from slowing down long enough to notice the human being in front of you.

Like the time I landed in Omaha during peak championship baseball season. It was over 100 degrees, humidity off the charts, and rental cars were scarce. I finally made it to the lot where a poor young woman stood outside, sweating through her uniform, name tag glinting in the sun: Trainee. I sympathized, saying it was a shame she had to work outside in the heat just because she was a trainee. She shot back: "That's Tră-nāy." Oops.

Embarrassing? Sure. But here's the point: ROI of time isn't only about efficiency. A two-minute chat, even a botched one, is an investment in kindness—and sometimes that's the best dividend you'll ever get.

### Using Lack of Time to Your Advantage

Most people treat lack of time as a handicap. I treat it like an edge. We live in an instant-gratification world—people don't want to learn, they want answers-on-demand. That's where preparation pays.

> Lack of time forced me to focus on learning that mattered.

For years I've read 20–25 business books a year, dug into articles, podcasts, webinars, even paid my own way to conferences just to meet people and learn. Result? When someone needs context, strategy, or a connection, I've already done the homework. I look like the "answer guy." Truth is, I just invested the time when no one else would.

The ROI is massive: knowledge compounds, relationships stack, and memory ties it together. Lack of time didn't slow me down—it forced me to focus on learning that actually mattered. And that turned into a reputation dividend I still cash today.

## Calendar as a Strategy Document

Every year we have performance reviews. I maintain detailed calendars—not as a "to do" list, but as a memoriam of how I actually spent my time during the last year. I have my work calendar and a separate life-family-nonwork calendar that includes my schedule of speaking engagement events globally.

When my boss wants to have the annual performance discussion, it's easy to assemble the work done over the past 12-15 months. I scan my calendar, assign activities to different categories and provide a representative list of tasks. No scrambling to figure out what I've done. It's all there in black and white.

Comparing my work calendar and activities to my person-family-nonwork gives me perspective on whether my life is in balance or if work is trying to creep up on my time and this allows me to make adjustments the following year. Right now things are in pretty good balance. It means I'm getting a good ROI on my time.

Think of this as a quarterly business review of your life. Ask the tough questions about where you want to spend time versus where you actually spend your time. You'll be glad you did.

## Compounding Small Pivots in Time

People think they need to blow up their life to make a change. Quit the job, sell the house, move to Fiji, buy the midlife-crisis Harley. We love the drama of the "big pivot." But the truth is, the ROI of time rarely comes from grand gestures. It comes from boring, almost invisible reallocations.

Fifteen minutes here. Thirty minutes there. That's where the magic recalibration takes place.

Reclaim thirty minutes a day and you're banking 180 hours a year. What would you do with that "extra" time? Health club schedule, more time with the kids and parents, reading, doing something that makes you happy. Stretch that over ten years and you've recouped 1,800 hours for yourself. That's six months of life redirected into something that compounds. Something that matters to you.

**Tilt your course by one degree toward the things that matter.**

Pilots know something called the 1-in-60 rule. If your heading is off by just one degree, you'll end up a mile off course after 60 miles. At first, that one degree feels like nothing—barely a twitch of the dial. But left unchecked, it compounds into getting lost.

Life works the same way. Fifteen minutes wasted here, thirty minutes ignored there. Rarely does it look like much. But stretch it over years, and suddenly you're miles from where you thought you'd be. Flip it to the positive, and the same rule makes you unstoppable. Tilt your course by one degree toward the things that matter, and ten years later you're living on a different continent, metaphorically speaking.

The same way compounding interest quietly builds wealth, compounding pivots quietly build a life. At first, it's just squeezing in a walk or reading a chapter before bed. But one day you look back and realize the walk added years to your health.

The alternative is just as true. Ignore the pivots and you start paying compound interest on regret. It doesn't happen in a day. It happens quietly while you were busy chasing "urgent."

Managing time is just like portfolio management. You diversify, rebalance, adjust. Same with time. Shave thirty minutes off email and reinvest it into mentoring someone. Trade one meeting for a walk with your spouse. Tilt the calendar just a degree or two. That's it! A degree today becomes a whole new direction ten years from now.

## A Life Well Traveled or Well Lived?

At the end of it all, ROI of time isn't measured in miles flown, hotel upgrades, or plaques on the wall. Those are just receipts. The real dividends are the dinners you didn't miss, the kids you showed up for, the moments that compounded into memories. When you look in the rearview mirror of your life, what ocean do you want to see? Red and crowded, or blue and wide open? The choice is yours ... and it starts with how you spend the next hour.

# key lessons

### 1. Urgent Things Scream; Important Things Whisper. Learn Which Voice Deserves Your Life.

Fire drills, pointless meetings, endless PowerPoints—they devour your time while adding nothing to your life's story.

Meanwhile, the important moments—birthdays, rehearsals, being present—almost never shout for attention.

Success comes from choosing the whispers. **You don't get those moments twice. Trust me.**

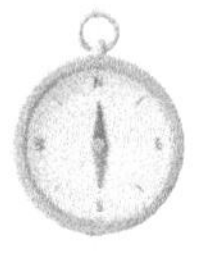

### 2. Micro-Pivots Create Macro-Change: The 1-Degree Rule Applies to Life as Much as Flight.

You don't need a dramatic life overhaul.

Fifteen minutes reclaimed each day becomes **180 hours a year.**

Shift your time one degree toward meaningful things and your life ends up in a different place entirely.

Small pivots result in massive trajectory changes over time. You'll wonder why you didn't do this before now.

### 3. Time Is Your Most Precious Currency and Most People Spend It Like It's Monopoly Money.

Miles, status, hotel tiers—they aren't achievements. They're tombstones for years traded away in the corporate carnival.

Once you finally realize **you can't earn time back,** everything shifts: what you say yes to, what you tolerate, what you prioritize.

Some people treat time like it's free.

But every "quick call," every "simple request," every "just hop on" comes with a hidden invoice.

Your strategy: say **yes with conditions.** *Make others choose what gets dropped so you can protect what matters —your time and your sanity.*

thirty two

# The Long Game

And are you playing the right game to get there?

If you woke up today, suddenly 21 years old again—with all the knowledge and insights you carry now—what would you do differently? Would you choose another career, another path? Or would you double down and do it all the same?

That's the classic philosophical thought experiment. But it's also practical. Today is the first day of the rest of your life. The only real question is: what game are you playing?

Chan Kim and Renée Mauborgne's *Blue Ocean Strategy* draws the map: red oceans are crowded, bloody markets. They are well-known and brutally competitive. Blue oceans are undiscovered waters: unexplored, unclaimed, full of risk and reward.

Careers work the same way. The red ocean is the corporate grind, predictable and defined. The blue ocean path is entrepreneurial: unknown, uncharted, sometimes terrifying, sometimes liberating. Both have advantages. Both have risks.

The choice is yours: red ocean or blue? Red pill or blue pill, if you prefer the Matrix metaphor.

This is where competitive intelligence turns inward. Apply the same analysis you'd use on rivals to yourself. What are your long-term goals? And are you playing the right game to get there?

### The Color Purple ... Not the Movie

You thought this was going to be another red vs. blue showdown? Nope. Life's not a political debate or an ocean battle. What, then, is it? It's a custom paint job. You mix your reds and blues, stir them around, and decide what shade of purple you want to wear.

Your "portfolio of life" has different asset classes, some red ocean, some blue. The trick of the long game isn't choosing one or the other—it's balancing both.

### Core Assets ... the Red Ocean

The red hue in your purple comes from the steady, stable choices you make: your job, your skills, your reputation. It's the pigment that gives your life color and doesn't fade easily. It's a reliable shade even when the lighting or canvas changes. It's your core. These core assets aren't always exciting, but they keep you grounded. Without them, you might feel like a raft drifting without any anchor available. Too much red, though, and your purple dulls and you get maroon instead: solid and dependable, but flat.

### Growth Assets ... the Blue Ocean

Blue is the spark, the edge, the boldness in your purple. This is your experimental and entrepreneurial leanings: starting a company, writing a book, mentoring someone who surprises you with his/her brilliance. This is where you test your imagination and the boundaries that might not be as rigid as you believed. It makes purple vivid and bright, almost electric. Blues can be side projects that can look absurd at times—those new ventures and odd bets, but blue is also volatile. Overdo it and your purple skews neon: thrilling at first, yet exhausting if you can't sustain it.

## Relational Assets ... the Purple

Red and blue fuse into something new. Relationships are the true purple in your life—family, friendships, mentorships, community. They're not just another asset class; they're the blend itself. I've learned the hard way that a career without these dividends end up empty, no matter how much red stability or blue excitement you stockpile. The joys of seeing the kids grow up, the moments with those who stuck with you throughout the chaos—that is the shade of purple that lasts. If you neglect this part, your purple washes out, and no amount of success in other areas can repaint it.

**The long game is knowing when to adjust the blend.**

## Liquidity & Optionality ... Shading and Contrast

Every artist knows it's not just the pigment that makes a painting, but light and contrast. Liquidity in life works the same way. It's your time, your energy, your ability to pivot. Without it, your purple gets stuck in one shade forever. The long game is having resources: money, skills, health, and relationships to remix when needed and bring the color pallet to life. A few years ago, I realized I was overcommitted in work and underinvested in flexibility. Shifting that balance gave the option to take new risks without blowing up what I'd already built.

### Risk Management & Rebalancing ... Remixing the Color

Purple isn't a fixed color; it changes as you remix over time. At 25, your purple might lean heavy red: stability, skills, proving yourself. At 40, you might add bold streaks of blue: side ventures, new passions. At 60, you start deepening the purple with relationships, mentoring, and building that legacy. The trick is rebalancing. If you never remix, you end up stuck with the wrong shade for the stage of life you're in. Too much red and you stagnate. Too much blue leads to chaos. Too little relationship purple leaves you with regret.

The long game is knowing when to adjust the blend.

### The Punchline ... Your Signature Shade

In the end, no two purples are alike. The exact shade you mix: how much red, how much blue, how deeply relational you make it—is your signature color. It's uniquely you. That's your long game.

Companies call it differentiation. Life calls it identity.

> The long game is about
> mixing your shade of purple.

When you look back, the question isn't whether you chose red or blue. It's whether you created a purple worth remembering—one that reflects the risks you took, the relationships you built, and the legacy you leave. That's the portfolio that compounds long after the market closes.

## Final Thoughts

So let's circle back. If you woke up 21 again, would you choose red or blue? The truth is that life was never about picking one. I found that out the hard way: The School or Hard Knocks. It was about blending them. The long game is about mixing your own shade of purple—one that is steady enough to keep you anchored, bold enough to keep you alive, and deep enough to carry relationships that make it matter.

That's the challenge and the invitation. Apply the same competitive intelligence you would use on rivals to yourself. It doesn't happen by chance … you must do it with intent and planning. Audit your portfolio. Rebalance the mix. Decide what shade of purple you want to paint across the decades. Because in the end, nobody remembers the buckets of red or blue you collected. What they remember is the purple you created, the unique signature that was unmistakably yours.

# Acknowledgments

First, my gratitude to God, for guidance and grace. I was extremely fortunate in my career to have learned from some of the best people in their respective fields like Greg Strouse who gave me my first break and taught me the art of product management, how to be a strategic thinker, and how to be a great boss. Others include Jim Holland, Frank Slootman, Greg Coticchia, Buff Jones, John Crossno, Myra Falisz, Jim and Susan Greenup, Steve Johnson, Jim Foxworthy, Jim Feeny, Jen Crowley, Gene Fukumoto, Paul O'Connor, David Kenyon, Jon Benson, Nigel Desseau, and others I've worked with and I'm honored to call friends and colleagues, thank you. I would not be where I am at or who I am without you having touched my life and career. A shout out to my first mentor who believed in me: thank you, Roger Loeb—you set my trajectory whether you knew it or not.

There were others early in my career who provided me with invaluable guidance and friendship that still are with me today. People like Dr. David Monarchi, Ann Erdenberger, Mike Mosher, Fred Haddock, Dave Kosmatka, Marc Staimer, Kengo Kuwamura, Koichi Onodera, and Mike Calderon were like the fletching's on my arrow providing me guidance that would keep my trajectory straight when I didn't know where or what the target was.

Professionals who have been with me throughout the latter journey: Camberley Bates, Phil Goodwin, Bob Amatruda, Jennie Buchwald, Peggy Ringhausen, Matt Coblentz, Pierre Hiller, Jason

Smith, David Jacobsen, Robert Bunchek, Arjan Singh, Fiona Schrader, Reggie Allen, and Tom Poole. I couldn't have done it without your steady presence and friendship.

Giants in the Competitive Intelligence community like Benjamin Gilad who has been a mentor (mensch), colleague, and most importantly, a friend. My colleagues who served with me on the SCIP Board of Advisors—Laurie Young, Maureen Nail, Avner Barnea, Christophe Bisson, Graeme Dixon, Lisa Hicks, and former SCIP Executive Director, Cam Mackey. A special thanks to Ellen Naylor—without her mentorship, guidance, and encouragement. Recognition to colleagues over the years—Dr. Boris Zibitsker, Kate Winkler, Dr. Claudia Imhoff, Dr. Craig Fleisher, Babette Bensoussan, Arik Johnson, Derek Johnson, Michelle Winter, Lisa Badolato, Amir Fleischman, Claudia Clayton, Alysse Nockels, Richard Caldwell, Lindy Smart, Cynthia Cheng Correia, August Jackson, Parmalee Eastman, Nan Bulger, Ben Scheerer, Tracy Berry, Luis Madureira, and Clara Smyth. A shout out to Wei Chen with CICI. PDMA colleagues Spike Ross-Corbett, Bill Reid, Chad McAllister, Matt Phillips, Sue Burek, Kristyn Corrigan, Mike Hyzy, and the great PDMA team at Ewald.

To scores of others, please forgive my failure to mention you by name. My life has been like a *Star Wars*™ movie with many talented actors who have contributed to the success of my life's screenplay. Listing everyone would be impossible. Plus, this isn't an Academy Award acceptance speech.

I would not be here either if not for my parents, Jack and Grayce, who raised me with the right value system, work principles, and a strong set of ethics. I come from a large family on my Mom's side—34 first cousins and other cousins once-and-twice removed (some forcibly) who influenced who I am. I am indebted to my

Dad's brother, Ed, who made a deal with me as a youth that he would happily pay for my Harvard tuition if I could get in—as a HBS graduate himself, he knew the rigor that was necessary for entrance and that this offer was a 100% safe bet. Uncle Ed was my first and most important life mentor on everything from school-to-business. I also wish to thank my in-laws, Ron and Kris, Sonny and Anne—they asked the right questions, gave sound advice, and gave me a beautiful, loving wife. And Sulee, my sister-in-law: friend, attorney, and advisor—thank you.

I was extremely fortunate to become associated with Dr. Judith Briles and her team in making this book a reality. Judith knows when to zig versus zag when publishing books, not to mention her sage advice which she generously shared. Judith and Rebecca Finkel took this from a manuscript, edited, proofed, added their magic, designed the book cover and layout, and played the critical role taking this book from a dream to getting it published. Judith is known as "The Book Shepherd"—an apt title—and she lives up to it in every way: thank you for guidance, support, and encouragement.

Behind every successful man is a great woman of strength and character, and that would be my wife and cornerstone of our family, Veronica. Our children: Mitchell, Evan, Grant, Monica, and Erik—thanks—you've made my life complete and I would do this all over again given the chance. You picked your mates well: Sierra, Jamie, Bryce, and Britainny—you are the kids I didn't have but now do; thank you for being a part of our family. Finally, my hopes for the future lay with my grandchildren Liam, Jorden, Oakley, Lincoln, and Remi—may all your dreams come true. You certainly completed mine.

xoxo

Papa Jay

# How to Work with Jay Nakagawa

Most speakers talk about strategy. Jay Nakagawa is a different type of strategy speaker. He has spent his career building it, testing it, and helping organizations win with it.

Today, he speaks globally on the future of competitive intelligence, strategy, innovation, and AI-enabled decision making—bringing a practitioner's perspective to audiences tired of theory without execution.

What makes his sessions different is simple: **He doesn't just study strategy .... *Instead, he builds the systems organizations use to compete.***

His talks connect the dots. He does it for his keynotes, executive briefings, leadership offsite retreats, workshops, panels, and masterclasses. He does it with his clearer way to think about competition; his practical ideas they can apply immediately; and a better understanding of how strategy actually succeeds inside organizations.

Great presentations have four essential components.

- Challenge how participants think.
- Give participants something they can use Monday morning.
- Outlast longer than any slide will.
- Change how participants see the game.

## Jay's Signature Keynotes

### The Future of Competitive Intelligence

How intelligence is evolving from research into a strategic operating capability.

### Seeing Around Corners

How great strategists develop pattern recognition and early warning capabilities competitors miss.

### AI and the Next Intelligence Revolution

How agent-based intelligence models will transform how organiztions compete.

### Why Smart Companies Still Get Surprised

Organizational blind spots and how intelligence teams prevent strategic failure.

### Strategy Is a Team Sport

How organizations build cultures that make better decisions faster.

### Innovation Without Guesswork

How structured thinking frameworks enable repeatable innovation.

### Invite Jay to Speak

Jay works with conference organizers and organizations looking for a keynote speaker who brings **enterprise credibility, intellectual depth, and practical strategic insight.**

For speaking availability:

**Jay Nakagawa** at **303-884-5004** or

**Jay@NakagawaGroup.com**

# Jay Nakagawa

...helps companies outsmart—
not just outspend—their competition.

Jay led Dell Technologies' global competitive intelligence (CI) function, transforming it into a strategic powerhouse that supports $100B in revenue and more than 50,000 stakeholders worldwide. His team of over 20 delivers market-shaping insights that influence billion-dollar decisions across product, sales, and corporate strategy.

With years of experience spanning product management, strategy, sales, development and marketing, he brings a cross-functional lens to every challenge. Whether it's war-gaming, product ideation, uncovering competitor blind spots, or influencing C-suite strategy, he's built a reputation for turning intelligence into action … and action into impact.

Recognized as a global thought leader and keynote speaker in Strategic Competitive Intelligence, Jay Nakagawa is passionate about helping organizations see around corners and make smarter, faster decisions in complex markets.

If you're looking how to sharpen your competitive edge, shape go-to-market strategy, or just swap war stories over coffee, he wants to connect.

Jay calls Colorado home and when he's not being an innovative disruptor for organizations and groups, you will find him either barbequing, with his grandkids, or blowing his trumpet.

in https://www.linkedin.com/in/jay-nakagawa-476395/

JayNakagawa.com • 303-884-5004 • Jay@NakagawaGroup.com

www.ingramcontent.com/pod-product-compliance
Ingram Content Group UK Ltd.
Pitfield, Milton Keynes, MK11 3LW, UK
UKHW062308290726
14090UKWH00018B/958

9 798993 587103